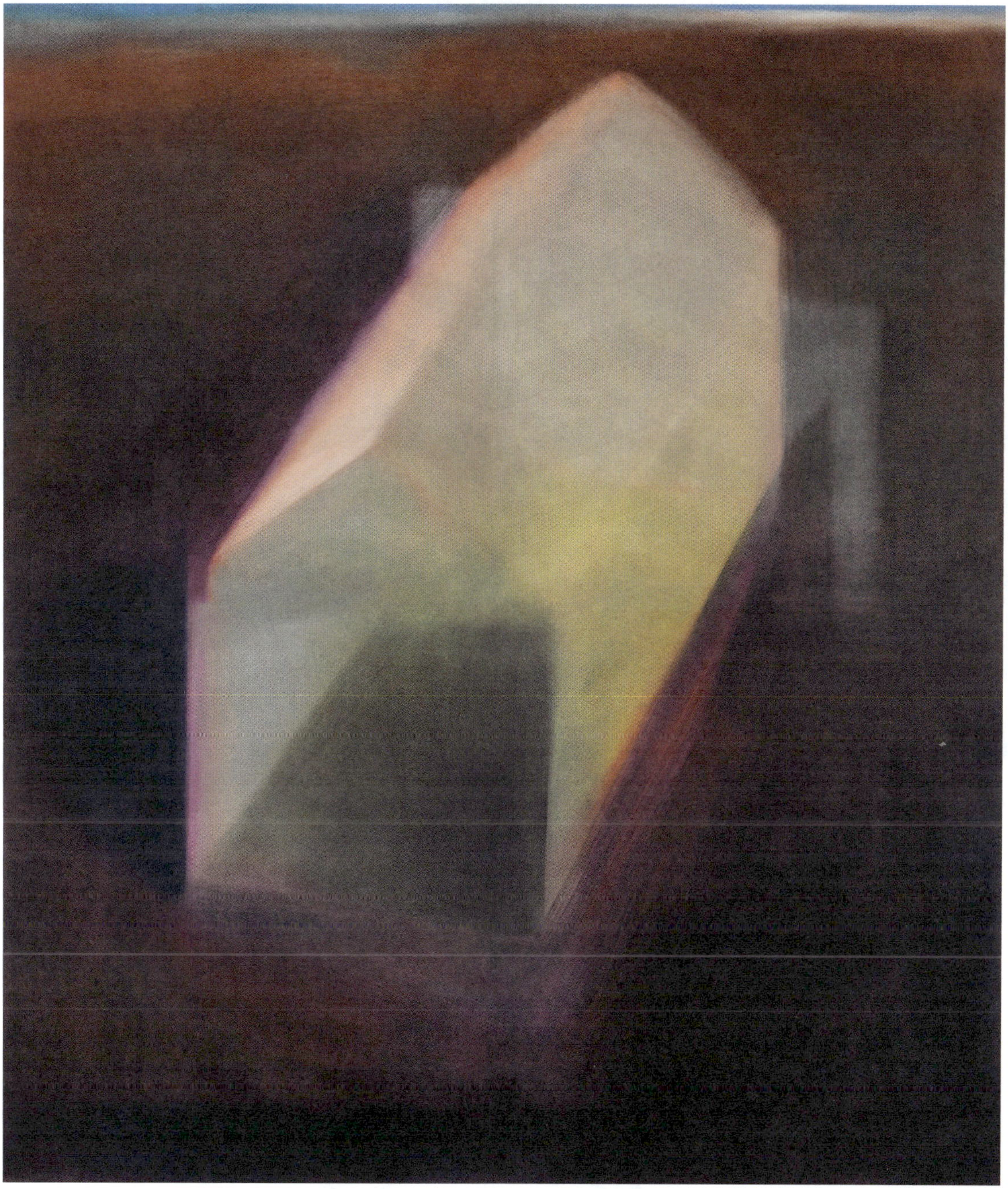

MIRIAM CAHN, *WEICHES HAUS*, 25.+26.10.11, OIL ON CANVAS, 78 3/4 X 68 7/8 INCHES /
COURTESY THE ARTIST, MEYER RIEGGER, BERLIN/KARLSRUHE

THIS ONE

& THIS ONE

THIS ONE TOO

EST. 1940

CHEVALIER'S BOOKS

126 N LARCHMONT BOULEVARD, LOS ANGELES, CA 90004
323-465-1334 | CHEVALIERSBOOKS.COM

LOS ANGELES REVIEW OF BOOKS

QUARTERLY JOURNAL // NO. 14 // LEGAL AFFAIRS EDITION

COVER ART
RAGEN MOSS FRONT: *UNTITLED (*SITE, OBJECT, STRUCTURE)*, 2014;
BACK: *SWEATSHIRT (WITH GRIDDED T-SHIRT)*, 2016

The Los Angeles Review of Books is a 501(c)(3) nonprofit organization. The *LARB Quarterly Journal* is published quarterly by the Los Angeles Review of Books, 6671 Sunset Blvd., Suite 1521, Los Angeles, CA 90028. Submissions for the *Journal* can be emailed to EDITORIAL@LAREVIEWOFBOOKS.ORG. Visit our website at WWW.LAREVIEWOFBOOKS.ORG.

The *LARB Quarterly Journal* is a premium of the LARB Membership Program. Annual subscriptions are available. Go to WWW.LAREVIEWOFBOOKS.ORG/MEMBERSHIP for more information or email MEMBERSHIP@LAREVIEWOFBOOKS.ORG.

Distribution through Publishers Group West. If you are a retailer and would like to order the *LARB Quarterly Journal*, call 800-788-3123 or email orderentry@perseusbooks.com.

To place an ad in the *LARB Quarterly Journal*, email ADSALES@LAREVIEWOFBOOKS.ORG.

CONTENTS

QUARTERLY JOURNAL // NO. 14 // LEGAL AFFAIRS EDITION

OPPOSITE PAGE: SETH ALVERSON, *CHAINLINK FENC*
WITH BLUE SKY, 2013, OIL ON CANVAS, 38 X 32 INCHE

Dear Reader,

We find ourselves, in the spring of 2017, in a moment when understanding our legal system seems particularly urgent. Discussions of the law, circuits, judges, appellate courts, and hearings are in the news daily. This is not new of course, but the abundance feels rare. We are usually content to let that machine run on its own, assuming casually, that it will continue to run without our personal interference.

This special issue of the LARB Quarterly Journal, then, is dedicated to some of the best pieces that have appeared in our Legal Affairs section throughout the years. Helmed by Don Franzen, the section has published some of the most prominent contemporary thinkers and practitioners of law in the United States, hosting discussions of the many difficult legal questions we face nationally and globally. You will see here critical and personal considerations around human rights, incarceration, and free speech, as well as a thorough look at the issues facing the Constitution, ranging from the language on the page to the prison we still maintain in Cuba.

Fortunately, times of political crisis often inspire engagement, curiosity, and a rare longing for visibility. We hope these pieces propel that urge forward.

Medaya Ocher
Managing Editor

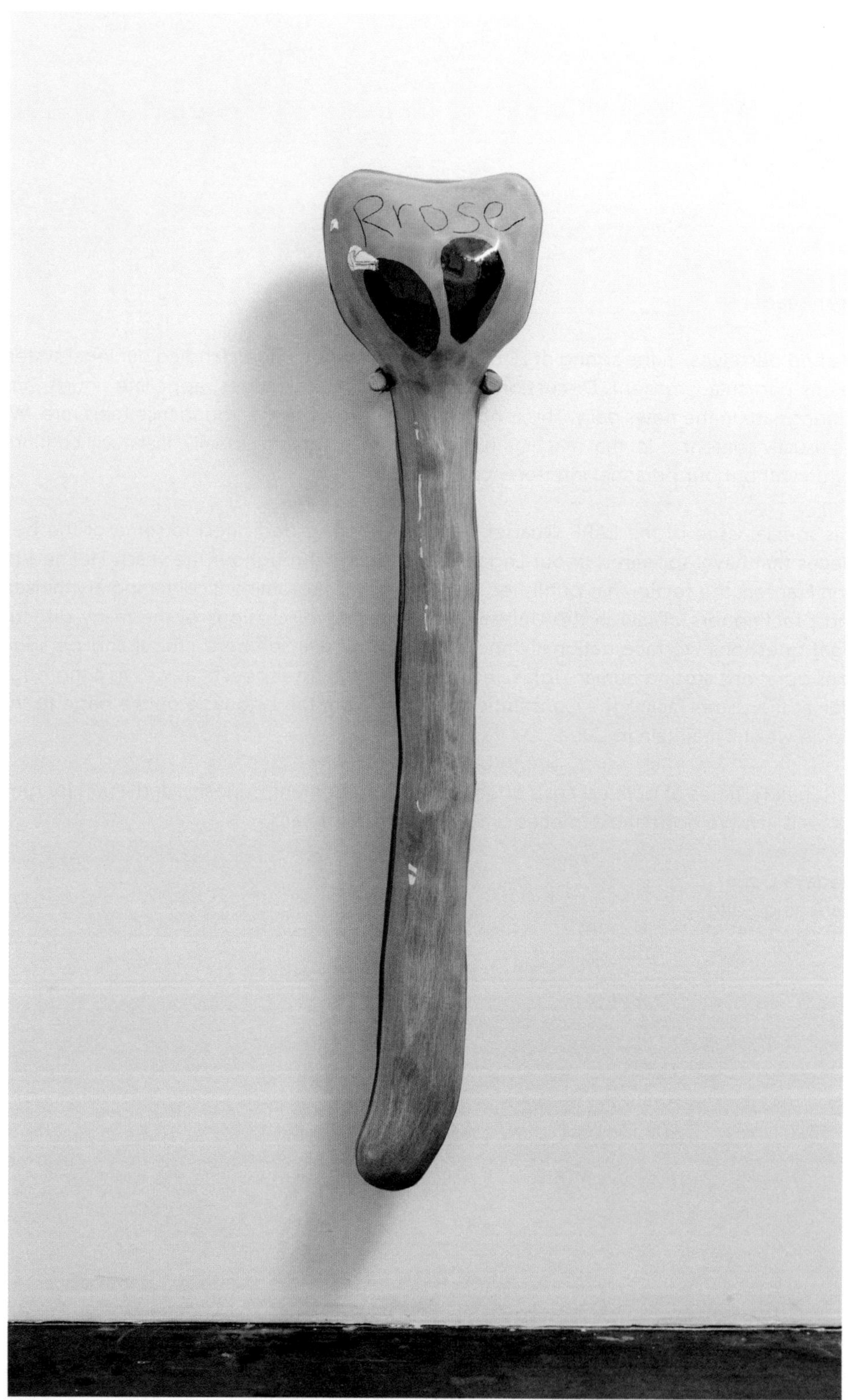

RAGEN MOSS, *RROSE*, 2016

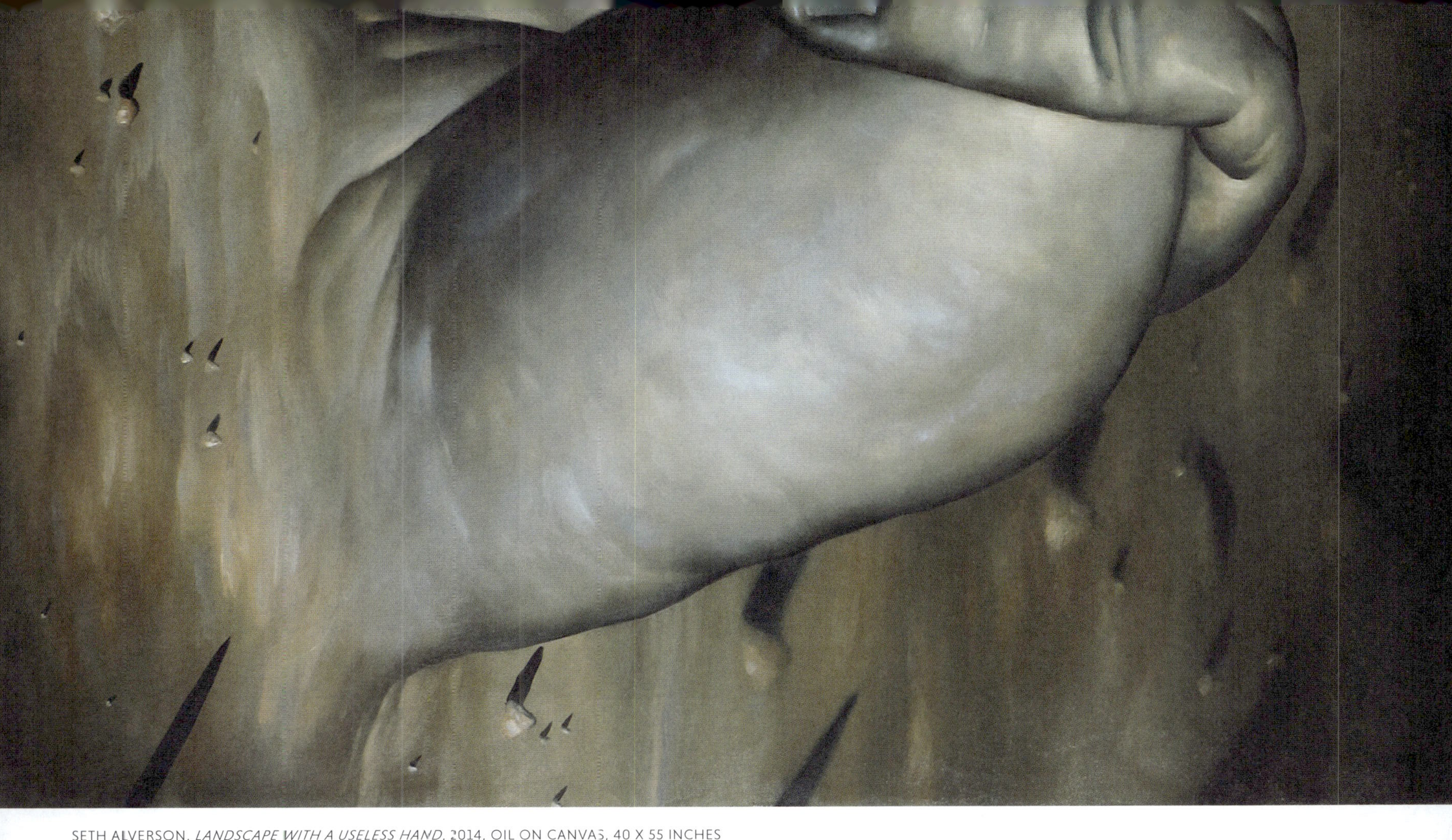

SETH ALVERSON, *LANDSCAPE WITH A USELESS HAND*, 2014, OIL ON CANVAS, 40 X 55 INCHES

ANNE LIBBY, *WINGED VICTORY (BEIGE SAND)*, 2015, HIGH-DENSITY POLYETHYLENE, POWDER COATED STEEL / COURTESY THE ARTIST AND NIGHT GALLERY / PHOTO: JEFF MCLANE

RAGEN MOSS, *UNTITLED (*MUSEUM)*, 2016

RAGEN MOSS, *UNTITLED (*MUSEUM)*, 2016 [REVERSE SIDE]

I.

CONSTITUTIONAL LAW

STATES IN A NATION

ERWIN CHEMERINSKY

PROFESSOR AKHIL REED AMAR has written a book that is simultaneously profound in its insights about the United States Constitution and quite frustrating for the reader. The book is filled with fascinating and important discussions of constitutional issues including state secession, the First Amendment and student speech, the Second Amendment and the right to bear arms, and the exclusionary rule as a remedy for Fourth Amendment violations. He discusses in detail how the composition of the Supreme Court has changed over time and provides a compelling account of Anthony Kennedy's role on the current Court. Amar's analysis is consistently original, and I learned a great deal from his clearly written discussion of these issues.

Amar does not present this as a collection of unconnected essays, instead organizing the discussion around 12 different states, each of which is used to introduce a topic. Chapter 1, for example, is titled "Illinois" and discusses Abraham Lincoln and his views on secession. Chapter 2 uses Alabama as the basis for discussing Hugo Black's contribution to constitutional law. Amar praises Justice Black and his contributions to constitutional law highly. Chapter 3 looks at New York and Justice Robert Jackson, and the way the backgrounds of the justices have changed over time. Chapter 4 is about California and Kennedy's importance on the Court. Chapter 5 concerns Kansas and *Brown v. Board of Education*. Chapter 6 is titled "Iowa," and focuses on student speech, because Iowa is where the landmark case *Tinker v. Des Moines Board of Education* arose. Chapter 7 is about Florida and the Supreme Court's terribly misguided decision in *Bush v. Gore*.

The last five chapters examine particular constitutional issues. Chapter 8 looks at Ohio and "Presidents without mandates" — those whose Electoral College tally was different than the popular vote totals, and those who assumed office after assassinations. Chapter 9 is about Texas and revisits Amar's prior writings about problems with presidential succession. Chapter 10 focuses on the Second Amendment and is titled "Wyoming." Finally, chapters 11 and 12, respectively, are about Massachusetts and New Jersey and present Amar's views about remedies for constitutional violations, especially recounting his long-standing criticism of the exclusionary rule as a remedy for police violations of the search and seizure protections provided by the Fourth Amendment.

Every chapter is filled with interesting and important analyses of these topics. But to a large extent, organizing the book around the states is artificial and irrelevant to Amar's discussion. For example, Amar's discussion of the Second Amendment is no more linked to Wyoming than to any other state where there is strong opposition to gun control. His discussion of how the composition of the Supreme Court has changed, and how the justices now all come from Harvard or Yale law schools and have a narrow range of experience, really has nothing to do with New York, the chapter in which it is found. Amar has been arguing against the exclusionary rule for years; it is not about Massachusetts in any particular way. The discussion of presidential succession is placed in a chapter about Texas only because Lyndon Johnson was sworn in there after John F. Kennedy's assassination; the issue of presidential succession has nothing specifically to do with Texas.

Occasionally, there are insights tied to a specific state. I found Amar's discussion of Lincoln's views on state secession particularly interesting. Amar explains that Lincoln believed that the nation preceded the existence of the states and that therefore states could not secede from it. Amar says that for someone like Robert E. Lee, who hailed from Virginia, "it was absurd to say that the Union came before the states." But for Lincoln, who was "born in Kentucky and moved to Indiana at age seven and then on to Illinois as a young man [...] it seemed natural that the Union came first logically and chronologically."

My concern, though, is not simply that organizing the book around specific states seems contrived, but that it begs the key question of the proper relationship between the states and the nation. Throughout American history, some of the most important constitutional battles have been fought in the name of "states' rights." In fact, virtually without exception, "states' rights" have been used by conservatives to oppose social progress.

In the early decades of the nation, Southerners opposed abolition of slavery by invoking states' rights and even claimed that state governments were sovereign and could interpose their sovereignty to nullify actions of the United States government. From the 1890s through 1936, the Supreme Court declared unconstitutional many progressive federal laws, such as the prohibition of the shipment in interstate commerce of goods made by child labor, based on states' rights. The New Deal was opposed on the grounds of states' rights and federalism. In the 1950s and 1960s, desegregation was opposed not by defending the morality and desirability of segregation but based on states' rights. Today, the primary argument advanced against a constitutional right to marriage equality for gays and lesbians is that the states should be able to decide this for themselves.

It is troubling that Amar writes the book as an homage to the states, but never acknowledges or discusses this disturbing history. The allocation of power between the national government and the state governments has been contested since the drafting of the Constitution in Philadelphia in 1787. Now, and always, the underlying issues have been about substantive outcomes: eliminating slavery, federal regulation of the economy, desegregation, marriage equality. Discussion of the states and the nation must take this into account.

There is one other aspect of Amar's book that I find frustrating, and it is the core of a disagreement that we have had for decades. Amar's approach to constitutional interpretation places great emphasis on the text of a provision and its history, with special emphasis on what was intended at the time a constitutional provision was adopted. He writes: "Sound interpretation of the Constitution often seeks to read the text as it was understood by the people who framed and ratified the language in question, or who reglossed it when adopting a later amendment." For example, his chapter on the exclusionary rule focuses on English history before the Constitution and argues that those who ratified the Fourth Amendment did not intend that evidence from illegal searches would be excluded from criminal trials.

In part, my criticism of Amar's methodology is based on his inconsistency. Amar expresses his strong support for a constitutional right to marriage equality. But in doing this, there is no mention of the text or the framers' intent, which obviously do not support such a constitutional right. Those who engage in originalism tend to do so when it yields the results they like. Antonin Scalia and Clarence Thomas use originalism to justify opposing the right to abortion or rights for gays and lesbians, but they ignore the original understanding when it comes to affirmative action where it was very clear that the framers of the Fourteenth Amendment meant to allow race-based remedies.

My larger criticism of Amar's methodology is that it ignores the importance of contemporary needs in interpreting the Constitution. The desirability of the exclusionary rule cannot be determined based solely on English law from the 18th century. The question is whether deterring police misconduct, and protecting people from being convicted because of it, justifies excluding illegally obtained evidence. If I were to debate Amar on the exclusionary rule, our arguments would go past each other. He would focus, as he does in chapter 11, on what the framers of the Fourth Amendment thought. I would argue about the need for the exclusionary rule in order to enforce the Fourth Amendment.

The Constitution was written for an agrarian, slave society. Those who drafted it, however brilliant, could not have imagined the world of the 21st century and the constitutional issues of these times. Their intent should be of limited import in constitutional interpretation. That is true of all parts of the Constitution. The Congress that ratified the Fourteenth Amendment also voted to segregate the District of Columbia public schools. But that surely does not mean that *Brown v. Board of Education* was wrongly decided.

Despite all of these concerns, Amar has written a fascinating book on constitutional history. I learned a great deal from it, as I believe will every reader. The underlying issues — the proper role of the states in the national government, the appropriate way to interpret the Constitution — will be argued over as long as the United States exists. Amar's new book has a great deal to say on these topics and is definitely worth reading.

ORIGINALLY PUBLISHED ON MAY 31, 2015

JIBADE-KHALIL HUFFMAN, *UNTITLED (DIPTYCH),*, 2013 ARCHIVAL INKJET PRINT, 31 X 23.75 INCHES / COURTESY OF THE ARTIST AND SAMUEL FREEMAN GALLERY

LAW AND DIPLOMACY

AKHIL REED AMAR

THESE ARE GOOD TIMES for Stephen Breyer. For most of his 21 years as a Supreme Court associate justice, he has been on the losing end of many of the biggest cases. But beginning with the Court's 5-4 decision upholding Obamacare in 2012, Breyer has won more than he has lost in the cases that matter most. In the last two years, he has generated his two greatest judicial opinions, and rarely in history has a justice made his most notable contributions this late in his time on the bench. After years of merely reacting to and counterpunching against an intellectual agenda defined largely by the Court's conservatives, led by Antonin Scalia and Clarence Thomas, Breyer has begun to shape an ambitious affirmative reform agenda of his own. And now, he has penned perhaps his best book, *The Court and the World.*

It is really four books in one. Each minibook is good, and one of the four — on justices as diplomats of sorts — is particularly provocative.

But before we get to the four minibooks, some general background and disclosure. I first met Stephen Breyer on the page, learning Administrative Law in 1982 from an outstanding casebook he had co-edited several years before as a Harvard Law School professor. The book wowed me, and the following year I applied to be his law clerk. (By that point, he had been named to a federal appellate court in Boston, while continuing to teach part time at Harvard — the man has always had tremendous energy.) When he offered me the job, I accepted immediately and enthusiastically. (There was only one other judge at the top of my wish list — a smart young appellate judge on the opposite coast named Anthony Kennedy.) Working for Breyer in 1984–85 was a wonderful experience. The judge was a remarkably generous boss, fun to talk to, filled with ideas, and amazingly quick on his feet. Discussing law with him was like playing lightning chess with a grandmaster. He helped me land my dream job in the legal academy and has remained a friend ever since. I admire him tremendously, and have sent many of my best students to clerk for him. We former clerks enjoy swapping stories about him, and while we sometimes poke fun at his quirks and foibles, our tales are always told with affection. No one who knows Stephen Breyer well has ever spoken ill of him. He is a mensch.

But that has never stopped me from critiquing his opinions — sometimes harshly — both to his face and in print. One of the things that I most admire about him is that he welcomes constructive criticism.

In that spirit, I must confess that until recently I am not sure that I could name a toweringly great Breyer opinion, an opinion for the ages. One reason is that he was often on the losing side, with few chances to speak for the Court in marquee cases. Long ago, when I complimented him on one particularly fine dissent that he had authored, he said nothing, but flashed a sad smile and held up four fingers. The game was to count to five, and in that case he had fallen one vote and one finger short.

But now things are looking up. Two terms ago, he penned his masterpiece in a case involving both administrative law, his first love, and constitutional law, the Court's main focus. The case, *Noel Canning*, implicated first principles of both substance and method. Never before had the Court issued a major ruling on the constitutional clause at issue — a clause concerning the president's power to make certain appointments unilaterally when the Senate is in recess. The case also pitted narrow literalism, championed by Justice Scalia (himself an Admin Law maven and former law prof) against Breyer's preferred interpretive method, emphasizing broader constitutional purpose and common sense, and reflecting deep respect for how the political branches of government have in fact operated and glossed the constitutional text over the centuries. Breyer's victory in *Noel Canning* was all the sweeter because Scalia had raised the stakes, doubling down with a fierce rebuttal. But this time — at last! — Breyer could raise a full five-fingered fist in triumph, backed as he was by his fellow liberals (Justices Ruth Bader Ginsburg, Sonia Sotomayor, and Elena Kagan) and also, critically, by swing Justice Anthony Kennedy.

If *Noel Canning* was Breyer's greatest triumph, another huge success quickly followed, in last term's Obamacare II case, captioned *King v. Burwell*. The case involved nice issues of statutory construction and administrative law — Breyer's wheelhouse. (In addition to being an Admin Law expert, he is a former congressional staff attorney.) And the Court's opinion — this time 6-3 — was classic Breyer, closely attentive to the overall structure of the statute, deeply respectful of Congress's main purpose, and impressively policy-wonkish in its grasp of this complicated enactment. And here's the kicker: not only did this classic Breyeresque opinion win the votes of Chief Justice John Roberts and swing Justice Anthony Kennedy, but Roberts himself wrote the opinion! Breyer has now gotten inside Roberts's head — the true measure of genuine intellectual influence — and in effect he got the Chief to write the very opinion he himself would have written. Once again, Justice Scalia was relegated to a dissent, gnashing his teeth and rending his toga in obvious frustration at being outmaneuvered.

Which brings us to Breyer's latest book, which is also aimed, albeit subtly, at Scalia. In 1997, Breyer and Scalia famously clashed, in a federalism case called *Printz*, about whether and how foreign constitutional law might be useful in interpreting the US Constitution. Breyer was on the losing end of that case; and in his new book, he generally purports to detour around this delicate subject. Instead he focuses on the role of foreign and international law: (1) in deciding national-security issues (which often involve persons and events beyond US shores); (2) in pondering whether various ambiguous American statutes are best read to regulate conduct outside the US; and (3) in construing federal treaties, which by their very nature implicate foreign governments — a.k.a. treaty partners. In all three contexts — in each of these three minibooks — Breyer skillfully shows that American courts must think carefully about foreign and international legal materials.

KARL HAENDEL, *THEME TIME - TEARS (HEAD ON HAND)*, 2014,
PENCIL ON PAPER WITH SHAPED FRAME, 43.75 X 45.75 X 2 INCHES FRAMED
/ COURTESY OF THE ARTIST, SUSANNE VIELMETTER LOS ANGELES PROJECTS,
AND MITCHELL-INNES & NASH, NY PHOTO: ROBERT WEDEMEYER

The indispensable role of foreign and international law in the context of extraterritorial statutes and treaties is almost self-evident; Breyer's main contribution here is to show in nice detail how non-American legal elements have interacted with American law in a wide range of actual Supreme Court cases, many of them cases in which he himself participated. The role of foreign and international law in domestic national-security cases is less self-evident, and here, Breyer makes a particularly nice move by highlighting the fact that the rights revolution in American case law — the Warren Court — roughly coincided with the 1948 Universal Declaration of Human Rights, the 1959 birth of the Human Rights Court in Strasbourg, and the emergence of strong constitutional courts in many advanced democracies outside the US.

Left largely unstated is Breyer's apparent premise that as American judges become more familiar with non-American legal sources in these three areas, these very same American jurists will naturally begin to think globally and to ponder foreign legal materials even in plain-vanilla cases of American constitutional law that do not directly involve foreign events or foreign persons —that is, in cases such as *Printz*.

Consider, for example, the death penalty. If state X wants to impose capital punishment on a certain kind of state resident — say a youthful offender or a low-IQ offender or an offender who did not himself pull the trigger — American courts do consider how many of state X's sister states would allow capital punishment in similar situations. But should American courts also consider the punishment practices of other civilized countries in deciding whether the death penalty in the American case at hand would be impermissibly cruel and unusual? In recent cases, the Court has indeed at times considered foreign-law practices, much to the delight of Justice Breyer and the disgust of Justice Scalia. Last term, Breyer wrote a separate opinion in a case called *Glossip*, raising the stakes dramatically by suggesting that perhaps all death penalties in America should be deemed unconstitutional. One fact favoring Breyer's new drift toward abolitionism is that many of the world's leading democracies have entirely abolished capital punishment within their own societies.

Breyer also uses his new book to subtly challenge Scalia on general interpretive method. The US Constitution does not itself contain a detailed set of instructions about whether it should be read literalistically à la Scalia or with greater attention to spirit and purpose à la Breyer. Nor do most congressional statutes specify just how much judges should emphasize context and general legislative purpose, or whether legislative history (Scalia's bête noir) should count for much. But in treaty law — the subject of Breyer's third minibook — there does exist a treaty that explicitly prescribes general rules for treaty interpretation. And this treaty on treaties — the Vienna Convention on the Law of Treaties — emphatically sides with Breyer against Scalia. It explicitly highlights the importance of a given treaty's overall "context in light of its object and purpose." It finds relevant "subsequent practice" above and beyond original intent. (This was a big theme of Breyer's in the non-treaty case of *Noel Canning*.) It expressly authorizes judges to consult key pieces of legislative history. To repeat, this treaty only governs treaty interpretation. But once American judges become increasingly comfortable with this sort of interpretive process in treaty cases, Breyer apparently believes (though he does not quite say, explicitly), that similar interpretive habits will carry over into plain vanilla cases of statutory and constitutional interpretation.

Perhaps the most interesting section of *The Court and The World* is its fourth and final minibook, "The Judge as Diplomat." If American judges increasingly engage foreign law and foreign judges, these judges in turn, Breyer argues, will likely pay more attention to American law, and thus America's soft power and influence will increase. On this view, diplomacy is not limited to presidents, ambassadors, and senators. Federal judges can also play their part in burnishing America's influence abroad.

It is an interesting argument, and also classic Breyer. He is a conversationalist par excellence and an extremely collegial jurist. He worked hard to befriend Sandra Day O'Connor in his early years on the Court, and now, perhaps, he is at last beginning to forge a bond with Chief Justice Roberts. Thus, with Breyer's fourth minibook he is once again bringing his ideas about domestic adjudication to bear on international and foreign-law matters. (Here, too, Justice Scalia is the anti-Breyer. Although Scalia can be utterly charming when he wants to be, at times he can be and has been — there is no nice way of saying this — a jerk. He alienated O'Connor at the same time Breyer wooed her. He has attacked Kennedy with special ferocity in a wide range of cases.)

But if Breyer is brilliant in pondering the possible significance of French law and Swiss law and English law and the law of many other modern democracies, he is less good at mastering the full constitutional history of America itself. They say the past is a foreign country. But this is a country that Breyer has not visited enough. He knows far less about the Founding and the Reconstruction than he should — and this is all the more unfortunate because there is a great deal of historical American material that in fact supports many of his best ideas. Good as it is, Breyer's latest book stumbles in its account of both the Civil War and the Revolution. (On the Civil War, he is too kind to Taney and too ungenerous to Lincoln; and as for the Revolutionary War, he conflates the 1783 Treaty of Paris with the very different 1814 Treaty of Ghent — a small slip in itself, but one that reflects his larger lack of mastery of American constitutional history.)

True, the past cannot be cajoled and befriended and charmed in the same way that Breyer can work his personal magic on his fellow justices or on foreign judges. Studying the past is less fun, perhaps, than seeing the sights in London and Paris. But to reach the next level of greatness, Stephen Breyer needs to visit the Founding and the Reconstruction.

ORIGINALLY PUBLISHED ON NOVEMBER 24, 2015

EL MOZOTE

WILLIAM ARCHILA

The photograph leads you to coarse lines
crooked along weathered grains
of a wooden tablet, probably painted

by a carpenter or wood cutter;
loops around the bowl whitewashed –
the color of clarity. Anacleta,

Amílcar, Macario. Characters branded
for a monument of wood & rock.
The morning the deer roamed

the thick of the woods, panels
of the sky capsized; the stare innocent,
the cut unclean. The bar, the stem,

the height. Cayetano, Candelaria,
Concepcion built like a house.
The sacristy burned

the way wood changes to fire.
Out of rubble fire. Femurs
afire. Like Milton's Late Massacre

they're outdated to the jury, robbed
of their own eyes, yet everything
is archived in the clouds. Doroteo,

Filomena, Facundo. Each name
a chamber, a chapel, fragment of a line
like an off-rhyme or a shotgun blast.

The only movement is the movement
of the monument. The contour,
the black metal. You turn the page

and the family rises. No arch, no thistle,
the town remained denuded of its residents,
many years the very picture lost in the hills.

Stunning, the number of shoes,
tricycles mangled. The absence
of the physical grace, the cadence

of a well-tuned body. The bending
& brushing. Insects, vessel-like roots
reaching for foliage; Zoila, Clicerio,

Olayo. Lines of a child. A minefield.

KARL HAENDEL, *THEME TIME - AROUND THE WORLD*, 2013, PENCIL AND ENAMEL ON PAPER, 51.5 X 76 X 1.5 INCHES FRAMED / COURTESY OF THE ARTIST, SUSANNE VIELMETTER LOS ANGELES PROJECTS, AND MITCHELL-INNES & NASH, NY / PHOTO: ROBERT WEDEMEYER

II.

CRIMINAL LAW AND JUSTICE

DOES THE PUNISHMENT FIT THE CRIME?

GIL GARCETTI

The history of crime and punishment across the millennia remains an inconsistent chronicle of experimentation, borrowing and adaptation, often dependent on time, place and history. The global history of crime and punishment remains a work in progress.

ON MY FIRST READING of *An Eye for an Eye*, Mitchel P. Roth's new book, I recall closing it and asking myself a series of questions: "What have I learned?," "How do I feel about what I had read?," "Was it worth my time and effort?" This book is not a quick read, not a book where you can quickly turn to the next page. Often you have to, and want to, ponder what you've just read. But if you are interested in the subject matter, or if you are a judge, lawyer, elected official, or a "student" of jurisprudence, reading this book will be worth your time and effort.

My dominant feeling was when I finished my first read of the book was disappointment — but it was not the content of the book that disappointed me. The book is the first I have read that attempts to chronicle and dispassionately explore the world history of crime and punishment. Professor Roth's effort is forceful, scholarly yet easily readable, informative, sometimes even entertainingly informative, and, lastly, provocative. Roth has said it was not written with the purpose of being a university textbook, but it easily could be the bones of a very interesting class for students of history or those interested in the law, government, philosophy, or criminology. The book is crammed with interesting facts and statistics and dozens of fascinating and sometimes gory anecdotes that have been brought together through disciplined and thorough research by the author (and probably others working with him). Roth, who teaches criminal justice and criminology at Sam Houston State University in Huntsville, Texas, has done an admirable job of scholarship.

My disappointment stemmed from the conclusion I drew, based on the facts Roth presents: that there is not one nation in the history of the world whose people, government, or rulers haven't been responsible for perpetrating horrific acts of cruelty, sadism, and savagery on other human beings. Is this the nature of man? Are we any safer today than 100, 500, 1,000, or 5,000 years ago? Roth could persuasively argue that we are indeed much safer — at least from the common street criminal. When you put aside acts of terrorism and accept that crime statistics in some countries are at best woefully inadequate, I think he is probably correct.

What Is A Crime?

Let us go back to the beginning. Roth gives us this definition of what constitutes a crime: "for the purposes of this book," he writes, "crime will be regarded as a legal concept, that is, what is or is not against the (written) law."

Happily, for those interested in the history of crime and punishment, Roth goes back thousands of years to the Chinese, Egyptians, Israelites, Babylonians, Mongols, and world tribe histories to share with us what constituted a crime before there were written laws. These were norms of expectations that citizens of communities or tribes were expected to follow. Communities created what I would call "community justice," sometimes very harsh and other times what would be called today "progressive." When laws were ultimately written they were laws that came from these cultures, social norms, and religious beliefs. Once written, most laws were viewed as rules that came from a god or prophet and needed to be obeyed without exception.

Roth makes clear how most groups borrowed from others in dealing with the issue of crime and justice. The Japanese borrowed from the Chinese, and many groups borrowed from the Egyptians, the Babylonians, and the Israelites. The English borrowed from their invaders, especially from the Romans and the Normans. We in the United States, of course, borrowed primarily from the English — the norm for former colonies of European states. But clearly each nation state establishes its own definitions of what constitutes a crime and what is an acceptable process of justice. What one entity may call a crime, another may call lawful. For example, in our own country, there are still 21 states that define adultery as a crime.

In reading *An Eye for an Eye*, what stood out for me was how early definitions of crimes were clearly biased against women, ethnic minorities, and the poor. Today we might have a more even and fair system of justice, but clearly some of the prejudices and unfairness still exist in our country as well as in others.

The timing of this book's release follows closely upon the publication of the Senate Intelligence Committee Report on the Central Intelligence Agency's program that resulted in the detention and torture of terrorism suspects after the September 11th attacks. Interestingly the banner headline of *The New York Times* did not use the word "torture"; it used the word "brutality." The editorial page in its lead editorial was not as lenient as the headline editors. The editorial page used the word that would have come to the mind of most Americans, "torture." The report would seem to prove that CIA agents and their agents tortured and sometimes wrongfully detained people who were viewed or suspected of being terrorist suspects. Some might play word games and call some of the forms of torture used by CIA agents and operatives, "enhanced interrogation techniques." Clearly, in my opinion, most Americans would view many of these "techniques" as acts of torture.

Chairwoman Senator Dianne Feinstein called the CIA acts "a stain on our values." But who is asking that someone, the Attorney General or a special prosecutor, review this conduct to determine whether criminal prosecution is warranted? Do the clear acts of torture establish a crime? If not, how will we be able to deter similar conduct the next time we have a terrorist attack in our country? These are questions that deserve answers. Perhaps the Patriot Act or some other federal law protects those who engaged in acts a majority of the committee concluded were torture. If so, you and I and the world should be made known of these laws and serious thought given to amending them.

Torture of course has not always been a criminal act; in fact, it has often been a juridical one — a central form of punishment meted out by the justice system.

What Is The Right Punishment?

Roth describes the horrific forms of torture and execution that man has perpetrated since the beginning of humankind — in every nation state and people of our world. Before becoming a photographer, I was in the Los Angeles County District Attorney's office for 32 years. In those 32 years I spoke with and interviewed hundreds of police officers, victims and witnesses of brutal crimes, lawyers, and medical examiners. Even with this experience, I was shocked by the descriptions of torture and executions Roth describes. And for what purpose were these means employed worldwide? Was it to gain information or a confession? Was it community retribution? Was it to deter similar acts by others? Most likely the answer to each question is a qualified "yes," but Roth doesn't address the effectiveness and reliability of those means for the ends sought.

We do know that most nation states were moving away from torture by the mid-18th century. We learn that torture was declared illegal first in Scotland and Prussia in 1740. Other nation states followed over the ensuing decades. When some of the nation states that had made torture illegal founded colonies in Africa, South and North America, the illegality of torture was overlooked or ignored.

The larger question for me is: what purpose does any punishment serve? Law school students learn in their criminal law class that the purposes of punishment for violating criminal laws are: Deterrence, Incapacitation, Retribution, Restitution, and Rehabilitation. Not all apply in every case. This is a subject that could take a separate essay on its own to properly discuss. Later in this essay I will address the ultimate criminal punishment a nation state could impose, the most extreme case of incapacitation, execution, and the purpose it is meant to serve.

Roth documents the change in both crime and punishment on a worldwide basis. In California we have substantially changed the so-called "Three Strikes" law that kept some felons in state prison on a life sentence. Through the recently passed Proposition 47, Californians have reduced some crimes from felonies to misdemeanors with the consequence of much more lenient punishments. We have also de-criminalized the possession of marijuana.

But there will be many more issues to address in years to come — issues that are both difficult and complex. For example, why are the vast majority of our citizens who are facing criminal charges people of color? We learn from Roth's book that laws were often formed by communities or written into law in order to protect the elite or at least to favor them. Hundreds of years later there are many segments of our communities who would argue that the law and justice system still greatly favor the rich or powerful and that people of color and poor people are treated more harshly and with less fairness. The book also does not try to address issues that will be coming to the front, like the fairness of an ex-convict forever having to bear the consequences of being a felon. When you cannot get a job or an apartment simply because you are a felon, what are the consequences to the felon and the community? Will punishment for his or her crime continue for a lifetime? Is that fair? Is society loading the dice against a convicted felon and greatly increasing the chances that this person will be forced to return to a life of crime because carrying the label of a "felon" makes it much more challenging to find a decent job and apartment or home?

¤

An Eye for an Eye is not written to address these questions. But the book does us all a great service in forcing these and other questions to the front — questions and issues that deserve serious thought, consideration, and action. And it spurred me to think and write about two subjects that weigh heavily for me: about the acts of on-duty police officers that result in the death of a citizen and, secondly, the death penalty.

When Is An Act Of A Police Officer A Crime?

The killing of Michael Brown by Ferguson city police officer Darren Wilson and the killing of Eric Garner by New York City police officer Daniel Pantaleo are the latest examples of the killing of an unarmed black man or woman in the United States.

The St. Louis County District Attorney chose to present the case to the Grand Jury rather than make the decision himself as to whether to prosecute Officer Wilson for the killing of Mr. Brown. In St. Louis County it takes the votes of at least nine of 12 grand jurors to return an indictment. We do not know how many, if any, grand jurors voted to indict Office Wilson and which charges they considered. But we do know the St. Louis Grand Jury declined to return an indictment.

The killing of Mr. Eric Garner, apparently due in part, if not in whole, to the use of a chokehold by NYPD officer Daniel Pantaleo, was also heard by a Grand Jury, this one in Staten Island. As in the Brown case the Grand Jury declined to initiate criminal charges against officer Pantaleo or any of the other officers involved in subduing and arresting Garner. In New York, at least 12 of a minimum of 16 grand jurors hearing all of the evidence presented to the Grand Jury must vote to indict. The vote of this grand jury has not been made public. In New York a Grand Jury is comprised of up to 23 grand jurors.

I was a member of the Los Angeles County District Attorney office from 1968 to 2000. I was the elected District Attorney for eight years, the second ranking deputy district attorney for four years, and in charge of a division of prosecutors and investigators whose exclusive responsibility was the review, investigation, and where appropriate, the prosecution of every police shooting resulting in the death or injury of a citizen by a police officer. I held that position for approximately six years. Many controversial police shooting cases, including for example the Euila Love case, were cases that this division handled (i.e., this division made the decision whether to seek criminal prosecution or decline criminal prosecution).

In Los Angeles County, criminal cases are rarely taken to the county Grand Jury for possible indictment. The usual practice is for the district attorney's office to either charge a criminal suspect with a crime or to formally decline to charge that person. If charges are brought, the case goes through what is called a preliminary hearing. The purpose of this hearing is for a judge to determine whether there is a strong suspicion that a crime has been committed and that the charged person is the one responsible for the crime. If the judge finds the requisite probable cause, the case is then set for trial. (If a Grand Jury returns an indictment, the case skips the

© GIL GARCETTI, *IRON: 9*

preliminary hearing and the case is set for trial.)

However, we have left out one key piece of the charging decision. At least in California, and I think most states, before charges can ethically be brought by either the prosecuting attorney's office or the Grand Jury, there must be an independent finding: 1. That there is sufficient evidence to prove that a crime has been committed; 2. That there is sufficient evidence that the accused is the person responsible for the crime; 3. That the admissible evidence is of such convincing force that it would warrant conviction of the crime(s) charged by a reasonable and objective fact finder after hearing all the evidence available at the time of charging and after considering the most plausible, reasonably foreseeable defense(s) inherent in the prosecution's evidence. If the prosecuting attorney or Grand Jury concludes that any of the three is lacking, then, ethically, the prosecution must be declined.

When it comes to decisions to prosecute, the usual response from the community is "THAT is the job of a jury. It is not the D.A.'s job to make that decision." But, at least in California, it is the legal and ethical responsibility of the District Attorney. Indeed the vast majority of police shootings in Los Angeles as well as in the country result in no criminal action against an officer who shoots and kills a citizen. Our system of justice, right or wrong, makes it exceedingly difficult to successfully prosecute a police officer in a shooting case, most of which involve split-second judgment calls occurring in heated encounters. Even when officers are charged in such cases, it is the exceedingly rare case that 12 jurors will vote to convict the police officer of the charged crime.

Some object to the District Attorney's office handling such cases because of what is seen as a conflict of interest. Prosecutors are seen as working hand in hand with police officers every day. The feeling of many community members is that the prosecutor really can't be fair and impartial. Whether that is true or not, we don't have time or space to explore. It is enough perhaps that such a perception is very strong, especially in the minority communities most affected by police shootings.

Is there an answer that would give the community and police a better sense or feeling of fairness that the current system might not be able to provide today? A recent editorial in *The New York Times* endorses the New York State Attorney General's position that all police shooting cases in the state should be the responsibility of the state Attorney General's office. I support this position.

Some District Attorneys would howl that their office properly, professionally, and ethically handles such cases. But we are dealing with a public perception by significant parts of our constituencies that because of their daily working relationship with the police, local district attorneys simply cannot be the fair, impartial, and professional prosecutors that these cases require and demand.

Even if this were to happen, it still leaves a question that I have never seen addressed, the ability of the local judge to sit as a totally fair and impartial jurist in a police officer shooting case that involves a split second decision by the accused officer.

While I endorse the idea of taking all cases involving alleged police misconduct from the local District Attorney's office, I surely wouldn't want to be the Attorney General who, by law, would now be charged to handle these cases. He or she might rue the day he or she argued for exclusive jurisdiction over police officer shooting cases. Still, I would prefer an elected official having the responsibility of making these decisions rather than a special prosecutor appointed by the Governor, Attorney General, or Court.

What Useful Societal Purpose Does The Death Penalty Serve?

Perhaps Roth's book gives us the best historical treatise on a governing body's ultimate power in cases where an individual is charged with a crime: the possibility that the accused could receive a sentence of death.

The oldest of what we today call "governments" have used execution as the ultimate form of punishment. To today's sensibilities, many early crimes punishable by death are shocking. Trespassing onto a farm and stealing a chicken or eggs has resulted in the thief being executed in more than one country. It didn't make any difference in the law that the thief was a youngster. Virtually every country in the world today outlaws such reprehensible punishments. If a woman committed adultery in the 18th century in the United States she could be executed (I have not seen any historical reference to a male adulterer being executed). Today 21 states still have anti-adultery laws but no convicted adulterer can be sentenced to death — well, at least not by a court of law! In fact, what we see today is a world that continues to move away from using the death penalty — though women convicted of adultery in some countries can still be executed, even today.

While the United States is slowly moving away from using the death penalty, we should be aware that our country was just behind China, Iran, Saudi Arabia, and Iraq in the number of persons executed between 2007–'12. Like countries in the rest of the world, our states continue to replace the death penalty with life imprisonment without the possibility of parole. Eighteen states no longer have the death penalty. In Colorado, Washington, and California, there are executive or legally mandated moratoria on the death penalty.

My basic question about the death penalty is simple. Is there any useful societal purpose for it? As District Attorney I implemented and supported the death penalty. While I was the District Attorney we ultimately sought the death penalty in about 22 percent of all cases where someone was eligible for the death penalty. While these were clearly "the worst of the worst," I wanted to believe that the death penalty had a higher purpose than revenge or retribution. I wanted to believe that the death penalty was a deterrent. I wanted to believe that the best way of protecting our citizens was to execute the convicted murderer. I felt no sympathy for the killer regardless of his circumstances. The horrors he or she had brought to his victims and their loved ones were always on my mind.

I was wrong about deterrence. Virtually all experts agree that there is no proof that the death penalty deters. I also now realize that the most reasonable and least expensive way to protect our citizens from these killers is to keep them in prison for the rest of their lives.

As of January 5, 2015, there are 749 condemned prisoners on California's Death Row. It is estimated that this incarceration alone costs taxpayers $137 million every year. As more convicted murderers are sentenced to death, the costs to taxpayers rise. If those 749 prisoners were sentenced to life in prison without any chance of parole, the costs to taxpayers would be an annual cost of approximately $11.5 million. That means that every year taxpayers would have

$125.5 million to be used for productive purposes such as keeping teachers on their jobs, police officers working to solve crime, or providing restitution to victims of crime.

Today we can expect that the vast majority of the 749 condemned prisoners will live, by prison standards, a luxury life until they die of natural causes. I do not believe we will see another state execution in California.

Why should we want this result even if it saves the taxpayer tens of millions of dollars every year? Our system of justice is built on the belief that it is better that one guilty man go free than to convict an innocent man. How many innocent men have been executed in our country? We do not know the answer, but each of us know that this has happened even if we can't name a case. We are talking about human nature, human mistake, and, yes, about people in power abusing the criminal justice system for their own purposes. We are reminded of this terrible history too often. Just weeks ago we learned that a 14-year-old boy, George Stinney, was executed for the murder of two girls — murders he did not commit.

Since 1973 there have been 150 people in the United States freed from death row. Virtually every month we read about the freeing of a person imprisoned for decades and who a judge now determines was wrongfully convicted. At least that person is alive to walk out of prison.

The witnesses, police, prosecutors, judges, or juries who fail to meet the ethical and moral obligations of our society are few. But even those who meet every expected norm and responsibility of our criminal justice system make mistakes. When I see 749 prisoners on California's death row, I know that there must be some who do not belong there. Understand me, the vast, overwhelming majority of prisoners sentenced to death in this state and by the state, never deserve to be released from prison. But I also know that humans make mistakes. Execute a wrongfully convicted citizen and we all lose.

I have answered the question I posed at the top of this section and now challenge you, the reader, to respond if you disagree with me. Perhaps you can teach me something I do not know or persuade me with your argument. If you think retribution in itself is sufficient in terms of a useful societal purpose, I ask but can we afford it? What do we gain from it? Having been intimately involved in the debate about the death penalty and having had firsthand experience with it, I must conclude that the death penalty has no useful societal purpose and that it should be replaced with a sentence of life in prison without the possibility of parole. As Roth's *An Eye for an Eye* shows us, history has brought us here.

ORIGINALLY PUBLISHED ON FEBRUARY 8, 2015

TURN LEFT OR GET SHOT

PRIYANKA KUMAR

THE LEGENDARY BIOLOGIST E. O. Wilson once said: "We are drowning in information, while starving for wisdom." While we are not exactly drowning in information on how government policy, racial profiling, and systemic mass incarceration have worked in concert to exacerbate racial tensions in the United States, there is now a wealth of such analysis available, and one has to wonder how and when wisdom will infiltrate policy in a meaningful way.

It is well known that, with over two million people in prison, the US has a disproportionately high prison population compared to other developed countries. In addition to providing an ethical imperative to downsize, Elizabeth Hinton gives us an economic one in her recent book *From the War on Poverty to the War on Crime: The Making of Mass Incarceration in America*, pointing out that the prison system costs American taxpayers $80 billion annually. An obvious solution would be to divert part of the resources that fatten the private subcontractors who run US prisons to job creation and social services for low-income Latino and African Americans — two groups at high risk of incarceration. So why hasn't that been done? Hinton argues that such an approach was tried, albeit halfheartedly, during the Kennedy and the Johnson administrations, but failed — not because it was inherently faulty, but in part because of the racist biases, overt or otherwise, of the people charged with implementing it.

Those racist biases may be in remission today, but they resurface reliably and with disheartening frequency. Among the shootings this summer was the police shooting of a 32-year-old black man, Philando Castile, during a traffic stop in Falcon Heights, Minnesota. Because of a video posted to Facebook by Castile's girlfriend, we know he was shot while reaching for his driver's license and registration. He tried to tell the officer he was carrying a gun with a legal permit, which the officer may have misinterpreted. That fatal misinterpretation goes to the root of the fear in the United States about what the embittered black male might do. It turns out that Castile, a school district cafeteria employee (recently turned supervisor), didn't quite fit the stereotype of the embittered black male. His girlfriend was a housekeeper at a hotel. As has been shown again and again, economically disadvantaged blacks are most commonly on the receiving end of police brutality. Castile had been pulled over so many times in the past for minor infractions (49 times in 13 years, according to *The New York Times*) that it sadly may not be so surprising that he got shot in the end.

President Obama has called police shootings "an American issue." Tragically, the day after Castile's shooting, a sniper — a black man — killed five police officers in Dallas, in an apparent act of retaliation. This is a moment in race relations when anxiety rules, when the police understandably feel as frustrated and cornered as their supposed victims, and when many well-meaning Americans fear what the next headline might bring.

¤

In her book, Hinton relates another moment, several decades back, when race-related anxiety had similarly peaked in the country. The Watts riots erupted during Lyndon Johnson's administration in 1965, sparked by a drunk driving arrest and rumors that the police had kicked a pregnant woman. It is telling that the riots occurred in an economically depressed neighborhood of Los Angeles — the city was then in the grips of residential segregation. Watts's residents were frustrated with record unemployment levels — "in Watts, as many as one in three people could not find work" — and the apathy of the officials whose job it was to care. Authorities responded by swarming the area with LAPD and National Guardsmen and enforcing a tight curfew in a zone "larger than the island of Manhattan." Those who disobeyed the curfew were arrested or paid with their lives. Hinton writes that law enforcement authorities put up one sign at the boundaries of South Central Los Angeles that read: "Turn Left or Get Shot." It is a chilling message, and one that black men continue to get today from the police, albeit in a more muted form.

I began to attend the University of Southern California a few years after yet another set of comparable riots in the city — the 1992 Rodney King riots — and the shadow of that event still lurked. USC has various community outreach efforts and its historic commitment to staying in South Los Angeles is commendable. Still, I experienced the university as an island of learning and privilege in an economically depressed sea. Living just two blocks from campus, in campus housing, I couldn't help noting the disparity between the lives of the neighborhood residents and the USC population. It may seem like a superfluous detail to mention that the local supermarket carried almost no vegetables, but that was just one more tacit nod to the stereotype that black folk eat fried chicken, and, maybe, waffles. Various strip malls near the university had been destroyed during the riots, and rumor had it that no decent supermarket would set up shop in the area thereafter.

As I noted in my review earlier this year, Michelle Alexander addressed the hidden racism against blacks since slavery in her book *The New Jim Crow*, and more specifically how incarceration has been used against them in a systemic way. Hinton acknowledges the "groundbreaking" nature of Alexander's book, but suggests we have to dig deeper to understand the true nature of the War on Crime. She argues that the country's incarceration plague began not with Reagan's War on Drugs, but that its roots go all the way back to a surprising source: Lyndon Johnson's social welfare program during the Civil Rights era.

Some of Johnson's signature "War on Poverty" initiatives, such as Head Start and Job Corps grew out of the Kennedy administration's "early childhood education and manpower development programs." The Kennedy administration began its delinquency prevention program as a forward-thinking measure, and Hinton explains that it was backed by academic research and included social scientists in policy discussions.

> Whereas the Kennedy administration launched these social welfare measures as crime control initiatives, Johnson presented his administration's attempt to suppress

the "social dynamite" in African American urban neighborhoods as a larger, more expansive fight against poverty.

Both administrations had good, hands-on ideas, from pre-K programs to vocational job training. So what went wrong?

For one, the commissions and people charged with empowering disadvantaged blacks were unable to get past their racist biases. The programs were not decentralized or entrusted to, say, local black organizations — not even those with stellar records of service. In addition, programs that address the roots of complex social problems need commitment and time to yield results, but the unfortunate circumstances of urban violence such as the Watts riots turned the public mood. After Americans saw images of the riots — including of Watts residents damaging businesses owned by absentee whites — public opinion soured. Johnson responded by taking a tougher stance against crime and changing his focus from the War on Poverty to the War on Crime.

Putting more and better-equipped law enforcement officers on the street is a visibly shiny route to public safety and it is no wonder politicians so often turn to this Band-Aid solution. Under Johnson, resources meant for social services were diverted to law enforcement and the trend intensified so much under Nixon that soon social services were given little more than lip service. Despite some good intentions during the Kennedy and Johnson administrations, impoverished blacks never got the sustained infrastructural support needed to transcend their ghetto handicap, and, instead, continued to experience racial prejudice, an opportunity deficit, and chronic unemployment.

From the War on Poverty to the War on Crime doesn't have the strong voice that makes *The New Jim Crow* such compelling reading, but, nonetheless, it is rich with details and synthesis that give the reader fresh insights into how the well-meaning policies of the Kennedy and Johnson eras went awry. Hinton quotes Johnson as telling state law enforcement planners in 1966: "If we wish to rid this country of crime, if we wish to stop hacking at its branches only, we must cut its roots and drain its swampy breeding ground, the slum." It is interesting to ponder Johnson's statement in light of what we know today. Greater police monitoring of black neighborhoods has resulted in stamping large numbers of black youths with criminal records, effectively shutting them out from robust participation in the economy and in society.

¤

Hinton details a 1967 cabinet meeting in which sniping was perceived as "a new and deadly development." It was acknowledged that the police responded to sniping by firing randomly and risking hundreds of civilian casualties and worse: "the danger of a riot degenerating into a guerrilla war." It turns out that the numbers of sniping incidents were inflated, but what was clear was that sniping targeted "symbols of police power." In the summer of 2016, sniping was used in a similar context — as a way to wage war against the police for perceived grievances. This is a troubling development, not the least because it distracts from the job of addressing hidden racism in the country.

Because of retaliatory incidents — such as the shootings of the five policemen in Dallas — the Black Lives Matter movement risks losing some gains it has made in public empathy and

JIBADE-KHALIL HUFFMAN, *UNTITLED (SKIM)*, 2013ARCHIVAL INKJET PRINT, 16 X 22.25 INCHES / COURTESY OF THE ARTIST AND SAMUEL FREEMAN GALLERY

in what could have become a national resolve to end racial profiling. Many a movement has fizzled, or a positive outcome has been delayed, when unexpected violence turns the tide of public opinion. In the '60s, National Guardsmen were called in to suppress unrest in areas such as Detroit, Chicago, and Watts. Hinton quotes one guardsman in Detroit as saying, "If we see anyone move, we shoot and ask questions later." Today, our officers have to challenge themselves to shun the racist, murderous attitudes of the past, while, of course, keeping their own safety in mind. It is true that police officers are being scrutinized more for actions that may be racially biased, but we are also finding out in many instances that after the brouhaha has died down, the officers in question are not actually being charged for their brutality.

Dallas's police chief David O. Brown — a black man — has suggested after the recent shootings, that the police force is asked to take on too much:

> Every societal failure, we put it off on the cops to solve. Not enough mental health funding, let the cop handle it. Not enough drug addiction funding, let's give it to the cops. Here in Dallas we got a loose dog problem. Let's have the cops chase loose dogs. Schools fail, give it to the cops. Seventy percent of the African-American community is being raised by single women. Let's give it to the cops to solve that as well.

It would be interesting to find out what kind of money Congress allocates today for, say, social services or job training, how much actually trickles down to those programs, and how those funds could be increased. A segment of the population reliably howls murder whenever a significant investment is made to social services. But no one protests when law enforcement acquires fancier helicopters. Our police officers obviously need to be equipped in the best way possible, but when the allocation of resources has historically been so skewed in favor of law enforcement that the man in the ghetto sees almost nothing, or at least not enough to help him overcome the handicaps of ghetto living, that also hurts police officers. In her book's introduction, Hinton writes, "states like California and Michigan spend more money on imprisoning young people than on educating them."

¤

In 1968, the Kerner Commission warned that "[i]n the absence of a major commitment of resources on the part of American political and economic institutions, 'sufficient to make a dramatic, visible impact on life in the urban ghetto,' [...] the nation would be plagued by crime, violence, and lasting inequality." Though Johnson had commissioned this report, he looked the other way. It goes without saying that Nixon also looked the other way. Instead, in the early '70s, the Nixon White House launched the ill-conceived High Impact program to reduce crime in eight cities with serious crime problems.

While reading Hinton's book, a reader might question: Why did supposedly targeted programs such as $160 million High Impact program fail so abysmally? For one, the Nixon-era War on Crime had corruption oozing out of its ears. The headquarters of LEAA (Law Enforcement Assistance Administration), the federal government's law enforcement consultant, got a luxurious remodel, including with an office with "modernist silver foil walls and a private bathroom" for its director, Jerris Leonard, a former member of "three all-white social clubs in Milwaukee." Funds dispersed to a state might inexplicably be siphoned off toward, say, a plane for a governor. Overall, significantly more money was spent on more policemen and more gizmos (helicopters,

TV monitors, etc.) than on support services for young black men and women. An independent evaluation by the National Security Center chastised the High Impact program as being an "irresponsible, ill-conceived and politically motivated effort to throw money at a social program."

Surprisingly, there have been no fundamental shifts in government policy to alleviate inner city problems, despite the documented failure of efforts such as targeted surveillance and heavy policing in impoverished black communities. Instead more prisons have been opened to shut in the ghetto's problem children. In Nixon's time, the boom in prison construction was based partly on what turned out to be incorrect census projections that young black men would become the fastest growing demographic in the country:

> At a time when a number of policymakers, criminal justice authorities, and public figures were calling for the termination of prisons amid a growing prisoners' rights movement, emphasizing instead community-based alternatives, the Nixon administration's drive to increase the nation's penal population seemed all the more regressive. "I am persuaded that the institutions of prison probably must end," U.S. district court judge James Doyle reflected in a 1972 ruling in Wisconsin. "In many respects it is intolerable within the United States as was the institution of slavery, equally brutalizing to all involved, equally toxic to the social system, equally subversive of the brotherhood of men, even more costly by some standards and probably less rational."

More recently, at the Democratic National Convention, Hillary Clinton said that our incarceration system needs an overhaul. Whether that is lip service to voters or whether, if she is elected president, she will put political will behind closing prisons, only time will tell. Republican presidential nominee Donald Trump, on the other hand, expressed his support for private prisons to political commentator Chris Matthews. Trump's assessment is that private prisons "work a lot better." Among his considerable base, Trump has stoked white racial identity — and the deportation of Muslims — without addressing realities on the ground, much less realities in the ghetto. American demographics are undeniably changing, and it is inevitable that the country already *looks* different. In this time of uncertainty, change, and adjustment, a graceful solution might be to think in terms of a post-racial society: a meritocracy that acknowledges our different cultures while fostering shared values. While Trump enjoys a bucket of fried chicken in his private plane (*The New York Times*), he would do well to consider how his privatization-works-just-fine approach to prison reform will move the country away from the dark legacy of the Nixon-era prison boom or reduce our annual $80 billion prison bill.

ORIGINALLY PUBLISHED ON SEPTEMBER 24, 2016

FEDERICO GARCÍA LORCA & THE ANGELS OF CELERY

JUAN FELIPE HERRERA

It is all green —
listen to me:

see that explosion of cloud & leopard
of rebel dove & desolate wheels on the zapped corner
you can sew it in — here with

60's buttons &
paisley patch & an asparagus wig from Ginsberg's supermarket
remember Whitman in there? That's him
call the crimson bull decorated in moon love & jasmine & afternoon clocks
call please you must do it you must do it now you must
see this see this in La Plaza of Viges where Mama Rumba was born

& her castanets of future sands & revolutionaries delirious
on the Río Grande Valley border escape ladders
& her belly timing the cosmos of Blacks & Spaniards so

we are here now Federico
we are scrubbing the ancient palaces with
your angels of celery your neon-neon heads ragged in Afro-Cubanismo
in Afro-Urban-Hip-Hop chekere bead

put it here smear it there
paste it out crawl into it & fold up the falling
with your ecstasy bodies of lily-shaped horns & daybreak blood

ANNE LIBBY, *WINGED VICTORY (BEIGE HDPE)*, 2015, HIGH-DENSITY POLYETHYLENE, POWDER COATED STEEL / COURTESY THE ARTIST AND NIGHT GALLERY / PHOTO: JEFF MCLANE

© GIL GARCETTI, *IRON: 1121*

III.

SUPREME COURT

READING THE TEXT: AN INTERVIEW WITH JUSTICE ANTONIN SCALIA OF THE U.S. SUPREME COURT

DON FRANZEN *interviews* **ANTONIN SCALIA**

ANTONIN SCALIA IS THE SENIOR Associate Justice of the United States Supreme Court — he was appointed in 1986 by President Ronald Reagan. Considered by many to be the intellectual center of the Supreme Court's right wing, Justice Scalia is known for his articulate, outspoken, and unapologetic views on the Constitution and Bill of Rights. Together with law professor and author Bryan A. Garner, he recently authored Reading Law, a treatise on his views on legal interpretation, published by Thompson/West (A review of Reading Law appears today in LARB).

Justice Scalia agreed to be interviewed for the Los Angeles Review of Books by its legal affairs editor Don Franzen, but with a few conditions. The interview had to be directly related to the book. Justice Scalia would not discuss cases that have been recently decided by the Court, cases that are pending before the Court, or topics that are either pending or are likely to come before the Court.

Mr. Franzen met with Justice Scalia in Los Angeles after the Justice had given a speech to a local bar organization. Wearing a dark suit, and with several deputy U.S. marshals in attendance, the 76-year-old jurist spoke with his accustomed clarity in an open and often affable manner about his views on the meaning of the constitution and the interpretation of laws.

¤

FRANZEN: Your Honor, there are already so many treatises written on interpreting text and canons of interpretation, why did you and your co-writer Professor Garner feel that it was time to write this book on "reading law"?

SCALIA: Oh, I don't think there are that many treatises. I believe that the last treatise that really went through the canons systematically is a hundred years old. The canons have simply been disregarded in recent years. Indeed, they've been run down by the academy. So, that's why we thought it was necessary to teach textualists — those who want to be textualists — how to do textualism. You can't do it without knowing what are the clues to the meaning of a text.

FRANZEN: I've had at least one appellate case that turned on a textual issue — whether or not a particular canon applied. It does seem the treatment of the canons in the cases is sort of haphazard.

SCALIA: They are simply not taught systematically in the law schools, and you're quite right to the extent that students learn them they learn them episodically — in this case, that case and so forth. And they ought to be taught systematically, I think.

FRANZEN: Should that be a class in law school?

SCALIA: I think there should certainly be a course on statutory interpretation, and more and more law schools have begun to have such courses. But none of them, as far as I know, go systematically through the canons, because there's no text that has them.

FRANZEN: You and Professor Garner of course are both advocates of "textualism," the idea that meaning is to be found in the governing text, and also for "originalism," that you are looking for the "meaning that the text has borne from its inception" — here, I'm quoting from the book. And of course you reject judicial speculation about either what the text means from content outside of the text or the "desirability of the consequences of the reading" — that's also from your introduction. Text of course governs, but what would you say to the argument that the ability to rely on the original meaning weakens over time? Is there a difference between applying textualism to a contract written in 2008 versus a document written in 1787?

SCALIA: No, it seems to me that the parties agreed to what they agreed to, and I don't know why it would be fair to give one side or the other a change in the obligations simply because of the passage of time. They said what they said, and they agreed to what they agreed to. I don't see how the antiquity of the text has any bearing on whether its proper to give it the meaning that the parties that drafted it — if it's a bilateral contract, or the public that received it, if it's a statute or an ordinance — understood it to mean.

FRANZEN: Some would be surprised to see that you actually argue against strict construction. In fact, you include strict construction in your list of thirteen fallacies. Most people think textualism, originalism, and strict construction are sort of a trinity.

SCALIA: I think strict construction gives a bad name to textualism. My approach is to give the text a reasonable meaning that it bore when it was adopted. For instance, if you interpret strictly the First Amendment, it would be the case that Congress could censor handwritten letters, because, strictly, it covers only freedom of speech and of the press. A handwritten letter is neither speech nor press. Come on, that's absurd, that's not the meaning of the First Amendment. The First Amendment reasonably understood is a guarantee of freedom of expression, whether handwritten or oral, or semaphore or burning a flag.

FRANZEN: Then what about the *Reno* case, extending it to the internet?

SCALIA: Of course. There's no reason why speech on the internet is not speech.

FRANZEN: Obviously the gentlemen in Philadelphia couldn't have imagined the existence of the internet, but you think that fair reading of their intent would be that speech embraces future technologies?

SCALIA: I mean the internet is speech. An example of how you could distort the First Amendment is *New York Times vs. Sullivan.* I mean, at the time the First Amendment was adopted, libel was not a permissible form of speech. You could be liable for slandering someone. The Warren Court just decided, well, it'd be better if the press could criticize political figures with impunity, so long as they had some reasonable basis. That may be a good idea, and the people of New York State could have amended their libel law to have that result. But what the Court simply did was to give the First Amendment a meaning that nobody, *nobody* ever ratified. Nobody ever said you could not hold the press liable for slander.

FRANZEN: Then in the *Gertz* decision it went on to constitutionalize defamation law even outside the realm of public figures.

SCALIA: All of this may well be a good idea, but the issue is whether it's a good idea that should have been imposed on the whole country by the courts or should have been left to democratic choice.

FRANZEN: In your introduction to *Reading Law* you referenced a book that we reviewed already, Judge Wilkinson's book *Cosmic Constitutional Theory.*

SCALIA: Yes, yes.

FRANZEN: And of course, as you know, he ends up being sort of a constitutional agnostic.

SCALIA: Agnostic is the word, exactly.

FRANZEN: He ends up saying he is against all theories. But he also argues, in the course of going through all the theories, that even originalism can be subverted and used as a tool for judicial activism.

SCALIA: It's quite true of course. I mean, any tool can be misapplied. The difference is that originalism does not invite the judge to apply his own predilections. Yes, he can do it under the cover of originalism but it doesn't invite him to do that. Whereas the other theories, purposivism or consequentialism, the judge asks himself what would be a good result. And of course the good result is the result that he would like. So, there's a great difference between a theory that can be abused — any theory can be abused — and a theory that *invites* abuse, that invites the personification of the law.

FRANZEN: The Ninth Amendment is one of the articles of the Constitution that is oftentimes perplexing to jurists. What should a judge do, when a statute or constitutional provision references something outside of its language? For example, in the Ninth Amendment, there is reference to rights retained by the people, but no enumeration of what those rights are.

SCALIA: He should apply the Ninth Amendment as it is written. And I apply it rigorously; I do not deny or disparage the existence of other rights in the sense of natural rights. That's what the framers meant by that. Just because we've listed some rights of the people here doesn't mean that we don't believe that people have other rights. And if you try to take them away, we will revolt. And a revolt will be justified. It was the framers' expression of their belief in natural law. But they did not put it in the charge of the courts to enforce.

Look, when I was in law school, if you had asked me what the Ninth Amendment was and my life depended upon it, I would be dead! Nobody ever used the Ninth Amendment for anything. Now, since those who have been using substantive due process have finally acknowledged that it's a contradiction in terms, it's silliness, it's converting a procedural guarantee into a substantive guarantee, they abandon that and they want to jump over to various other devices to enable the courts to do what the courts would like to do. One of those devices is the Ninth Amendment. But that's not what the framers meant by it. All they meant by it was: I do not deny or disparage the right to abortion, for example. I know that it's not one of the rights protected by the Bill of Rights but I don't deny or disparage it. If people want to argue there is a natural right of a woman to have an abortion, that's fine. The mere fact that its not included in the Bill of Rights doesn't mean that it doesn't exist. But just don't ask me to enforce it.

FRANZEN: So you're just saying its not the province of the courts.

SCALIA: Right, if you believe it is a compendium of all unenumerated rights, you have to believe that the framers were nuts. I mean, did they go through the trouble of listing in detail, you know, the right to trial by jury in all matters of common law involving more than 20 dollars, no quartering of troops in homes, or one after another, and finally when you go, "yes, what should we add? Everything else." That's not the way you write a legal document. And this was a legal document. Just as the Tenth Amendment is nothing but an expression of the belief in federalism, so also the Ninth Amendment is nothing but an expression of belief in the natural law. But it is not an invitation to the judges to apply whatever they think the natural law says.

FRANZEN: As I went through your book there were a lot of fabulous quotations — *bon mots,* I would say. I especially enjoyed, for example, A.P. Herbert's fictional Lord Mildew who said, "if Parliament does not mean what it says, it must say so." I thought that was great.

SCALIA: It's a good one.

FRANZEN: So I was so impressed by the research in the book — how did you and Professor Garner assemble all this material?

SCALIA: I could not have done this book without the assistance of Bryan Garner because I could not use my own law clerks for the research on it. Bryan is a professor, and he has student assistants. They dug up some of the examples of cases. And he also has a substantial staff at LawProse, which is his company. These are seasoned lawyers, some of them nine years out, seven years out and so forth. And those people dug up most of the case examples. You know, Bryan and I reviewed them, and threw out a lot of them, and revised the description of some others. But that's how we were able to put it together. I couldn't have done it personally, nor could Bryan have done it personally.

FRANZEN: Well, there's tremendous scholarship in there. A lot of the canons of interpretation, of course, have their roots in Roman law. And [there are] lots of Roman maxims throughout the book.

SCALIA: Ah, you know why? Because it's common sense. Most of them are just common sense. So of course they would have been expressed in Latin, probably were expressed in Greek, I don't know.

FRANZEN: I even saw a citation to *Justinian's Digest* — I haven't seen one of those lately. But I wonder, do you think, did the Romans really sum up the principles of interpretation, or do you see a contribution from the English common law courts on this subject?

SCALIA: Oh, I don't think all of these canons are traceable to Roman law. I think probably most of them are developments of the common law courts — probably most of them.

FRANZEN: It seems that you draw distinction between the English common law, where, as you've explained, judges had almost a legislative power, versus the common law tradition in the United States. How do you think that is playing out in our judicial system?

SCALIA: Well that's very interesting. You know, our common law courts originally adhered to the English system that I describe, and once they found the common law, it couldn't be changed except by the legislature. It was about in the 1840s that you had the first American cases that say, "when the reason for the law changes, the law itself changes"— you know that maxim — and the common law courts feel the power to change the common law. That was something new. That also happens to be the time, and I don't think it's an accident, when the Americans began to elect their judges. Because seeing the great power that the judges had to change the law, they probably felt a need for more democratic input into the system.

FRANZEN: It's interesting that you mention that particular principle — "where the reason for the rule ceases so the rule should cease." That was the favorite adage of the first lawyer I worked for. He was a Harvard Law graduate and did a lot of constitutional litigation. I heard that rule cited every day. It's not mentioned anywhere in your book. Is it a canon of interpretation or would you say that maybe it should be included in the fallacies?

SCALIA: Well, it's obviously an adage that applies to the lawmaker, not to the law interpreter. A legislator should be aware of the fact that when a reason for a law is eliminated, the law itself should be abolished, or the law itself should be altered. And so should a judge be aware of that, if a judge is acting in a common law capacity and making the law. But it's rare in modern times that judges make the law, even in states where judges still have common law powers. Most of the law is codified, and the judge is almost always dealing with a text. And it certainly is not true with respect to a text — that when the reason for the text disappears, you can ignore the text, or rewrite the text, or distort the text. Nobody ever thought that was a principle applicable to textual interpretation; it was applicable to lawmaking, common law lawmaking.

FRANZEN: A lot of your canons are often cited in the cases and received principles of interpretation, such as the text must be construed as a whole. But you list 13 fallacies, and I

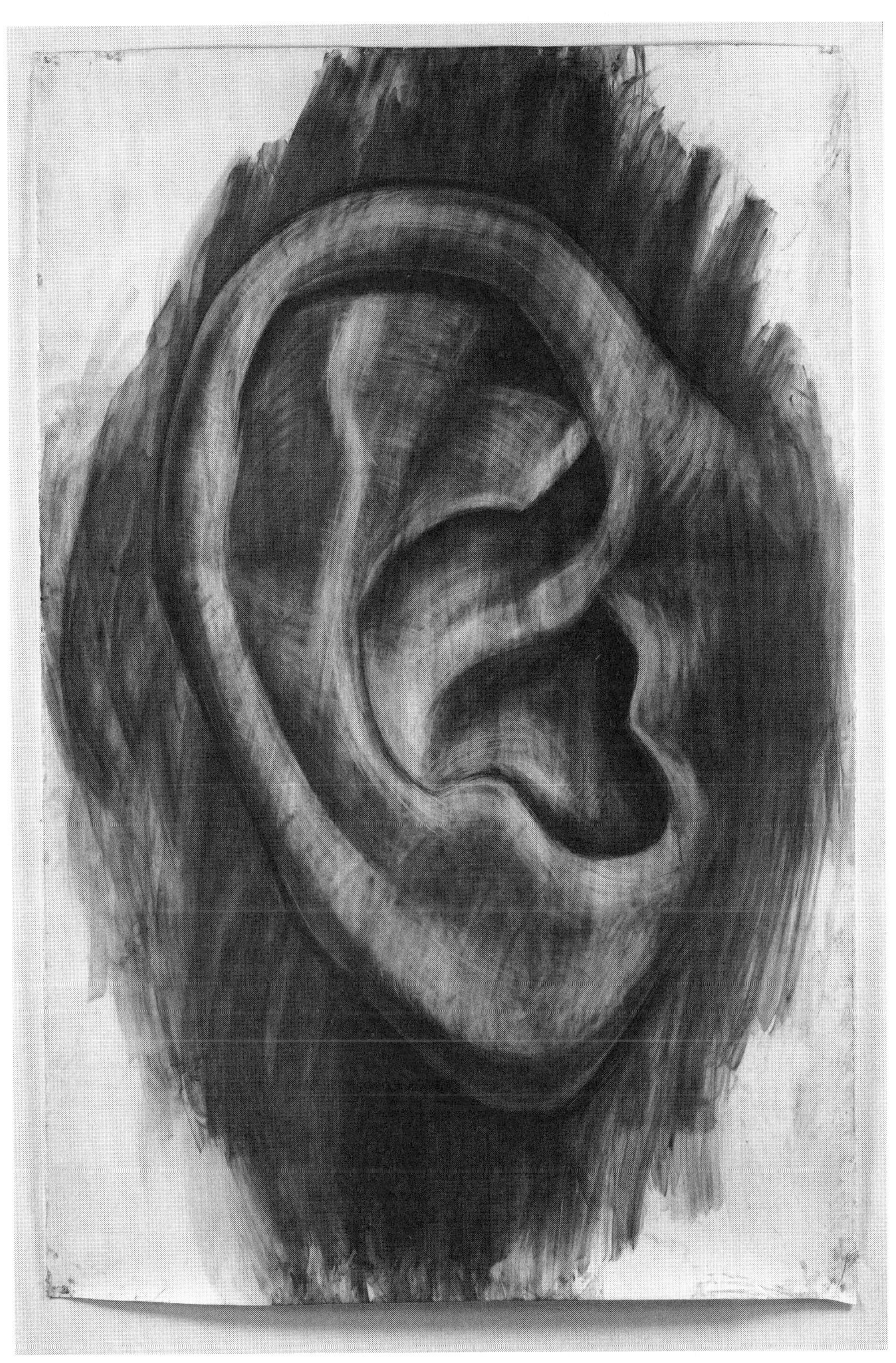

KARL HAENDEL, *LARGE EAR*, 2011, CHARCOAL ON PAPER, 77.5 X 52 / COURTESY OF THE ARTIST, SUSANNE VIELMETTER LOS ANGELES PROJECTS, AND MITCHELL-INNES & NASH, NY / PHOTO: ROBERT WEDEMEYER

want to ask you how you came up with that number. Was that just a coincidence?

SCALIA: Ah, you know, Bryan didn't like that, he wanted to either invent a fourteenth — but it is what it is.

FRANZEN: A number of those 13 are open to debate. For example, what you call the "false notion that the spirit of the law should prevail over the letter." There must certainly be people who take issue with that.

SCALIA: Oh, undoubtedly!

FRANZEN: Or "that the quest of interpretation is to do justice"— many would say that is not a fallacy. So, here it seems that you and Professor Garner are arguing a case as opposed to condensing law. Would you agree?

SCALIA: Oh, we say that early on in the book, in the introduction I think, that this book purports to be normative, not descriptive. Normative, what the law ought to be. And thus we reject some canons that are often expressed, such as "the spirit of the law prevails over the letter." Courts say that sometimes, but that's not a proper role for non-common law courts.

FRANZEN: Well, perhaps the fourteenth fallacy would be "where the reason for the rule ends the rule ends." In the revised edition you might want to add that!

SCALIA: We might want to add that — we could avoid unlucky thirteen!

FRANZEN: That maxim actually is in the *California Civil Code.*

SCALIA: Is it really?

FRANZEN: Yes, *Civil Code* Section 3510.

SCALIA: But does it govern enacted laws? I doubt it. I doubt whether the California courts ever said that because of this provision of the code, we can disregard statutes because we think times have changed and the reason.

FRANZEN: It's not cited very much but it is in the code. It's under a section called Maxims of Jurisprudence, where they list maxims, including some of the ones that are in your book.

SCALIA: Let me note that down, we should probably have a section on when the reason for the law ceases to exist so does the law itself.

FRANZEN: So you would say that on the issue of the fallacies that you put together, that is something where the law isn't settled, you're arguing a case there.

SCALIA: Sir, the law is not settled on textualism! I mean, of course the whole book is normative, it argues the case for textualism again, against whatever crazy system you want to replace it with, all of which boils down to the judge doing what he thinks is a good idea.

That's not descriptive, it's normative, and so also throughout the book we don't purport to be describing what all the courts do, but describing what they should do.

FRANZEN: What do you hope the impact of *Reading Law* will be?

SCALIA: I obviously hope that every judge will read it, and be persuaded of the correctness of treating text as democratically adopted text. And, you know, whether that will be so or not, I'm not sure. I am much more confident that a lot of lawyers will use the book because, as I said earlier, there is no other place where you can find all of the canons set forth unless you want to go back one hundred years. And they are useful to lawyers — whatever side you're arguing, there's usually some canon on your side. So I think lawyers will certainly use a lot of it. I hope judges will.

FRANZEN: Well, we have two copies in our office now, so we will definitely use it. Just a last line of questions — like you, I'm a great opera lover and I couldn't help but wonder as I went through the canons of interpretation and thought about originalism and textualism — do these principles, in your view, have any application to the performing arts? Is there a doctrine of originalism, say, applied to Wagner's *Ring Cycle*? Should we be trying to follow Wagner's original intent? Should we be applying textualism to Verdi?

SCALIA: Oh, I would probably be an originalist in the arts as well, and its not just opera, even in symphonic music. Do you follow Beethoven's notations, or as an artist yourself, if you're the conductor, do you improve upon them? That's always a controversy among artists, I think. And for myself I generally do not like taking liberties with the original.

FRANZEN: Well, maybe that can be a fifteenth fallacy — to apply a "living constitutionalist" approach to opera.

SCALIA: Although, I'll tell you, I can't say I always hate it. There was a production of *La Bohème* by the Washington company which was quite avant-garde, and the scene at the café where Musetta's waltz, it's a bar room that looks like the bar scene from *Star Wars*, there's all these really crazy characters in the place. Now, I thought it was wonderful. Ruth [Bader Ginsburg] hated it, Ruth hated it!

FRANZEN: Well, that's interesting, so maybe she's an originalist when it comes to opera.

SCALIA: I don't know, maybe, maybe.

FRANZEN: And you switch places when it comes to the arts!
Well thank you very much, Justice, for your time.

SCALIA: Thank you, I enjoyed talking to you.

ORIGINALLY PUBLISHED ON OCTOBER 1, 2012

A VALENTINE FOR A JUSTICE

LAURA W. BRILL

THOSE OF US who have admired Justice Ruth Bader Ginsburg for years and who have worked with her have always known her as a fierce and brilliant thinker. Fierce and brilliant thinkers normally toil in relative obscurity, at least when compared with the likes of Jay-Z and the Kardashians. This is why the *Notorious RBG* phenomenon took us as a surprise, though definitely a heartening and happy one.

Notorious RBG: The Life and Times of Ruth Bader Ginsburg is a loving, slightly ironic biographical gift-book that is a spin-off from a Tumblr fan site that launched Justice Ginsburg into the pop culture stratosphere. The book was written by the Tumblr creator, recent NYU Law grad Shana Knizhnik, and TV reporter Irin Carmon, who interviewed the Justice for MSNBC.

Picking it up, I wondered whether the two self-proclaimed #millennial authors would be more enamored with the "Notorious RBG" phenomenon that they created than with the actual Justice and her work. Would they reduce their story to a charming mash-up between an American story of a Jewish girl from Brooklyn who works hard and follows her dream to the US Supreme Court and the in-your-face energy of the rap music world? Or would they take their task more seriously, and attempt a deeper level of education?

The Supreme Court is an institution that takes its own solemnity very seriously. The internal deliberations of the justices are completely secret. Cameras are not allowed in the courtroom, lest legal advocacy veer into media grandstanding. Justices generally decline requests to participate in the news talk show circuit to pump up popular support for their rulings.

In fact, the range of action that a single justice can take if she sees the majority of her colleagues creating legal doctrine that steers the country in the wrong direction is quite limited.

She can write a dissent. She can explain what is wrong and why and what the likely consequences might be. She can point to areas of faulty or slippery reasoning. She can urge legislation to amend statutes that have been misconstrued. She can urge a different understanding of the constitution or even assert the need for an amendment if history proves necessary. And if the bare words on a written page seem too small for the deed, what else is there to do? Not much beyond taking to the bench, reading her views out loud, and donning a special garment to show she really means it.

These efforts of dissent are of little effect, however, unless the rest of us sit up, take notice, and do something.

No justice has a marketing team to amplify her voice. *Notorious RBG* steps into this void. It serves as a happy, amusing, and diverting megaphone, developing what the Tumblr started. It lets us know what Justice Ginsburg thinks is going wrong and why, and spreads her message, transforming Justice Ginsburg into a cultural icon, as fierce and unflappable as any legal thinker could be.

To those of us who knew the Justice before her face could be found on tattoos and T-shirts, and before babies thought of impersonating her for Halloween, her quiet brilliance, forceful conviction, and wit so dry it is often missed may have seemed unlikely to propel her to this status. Yet *Notorious RBG* teaches us that it is precisely these characteristics that make her an ideal personification of dissent. When the Supreme Court makes razor-thin majority rulings that are contrary to core principles of equality and that turn a blind eye to history, it is fitting that we should have images (the Justice's stylized face and big glasses) and slogans (you can't spell truth without Ruth) to help spread the word that something must be done.

The book is clearly a valentine. We see the Justice as part Thurgood Marshall, part Jackie O., and part your quiet but firm mother, grandmother, or sister, who will not be underestimated and who won't let you get away with anything, either.

The Notorious RBG concept takes on a superhero quality, but instead of the cape and tights, our hero dons a black robe, a jaunty gold crown, and a "dissent jabot" — the decorative collar she wears for appearances on the bench when she is reading from her dissent aloud for special emphasis and as a call to action against grave injustice.

For those looking for a more up-close-and-personal insight into the Justice, the authors provide a glimpse of that as well. We see wonderful photographs of the Justice as a child and as a young lawyer, toiling away for gender equality. Much of the biographical information has appeared in other settings but is presented in a breezy and appealing style, rather than a scholarly slog

Some of the tales remind us that it was not so long ago that the barriers women faced in the workplace often came in the form of fixed rules of exclusion. Her law school dean at Harvard polled the few women in the class to find out how they could justify taking a place from a man. When she sought to spend her last year of law school in New York to be with her husband Marty, who was recovering from cancer and had secured a position working as a tax attorney at a New York law firm, Harvard refused to grant her a degree, creating for Columbia Law School one very loyal alumna. But even graduation at the top of her class from Columbia could not in those days lead to a law firm position for the women graduates, RBG included.

Some of the stories remind us of the importance of good health and exercise. We learn of

MIRIAM CAHN, *MENSTRUATIONSHAUS*, M. 08.1982, CHALK ON VELLUM, 145 5/8 X 212 5/8 INCHES / COURTESY THE ARTIST, MEYER RIEGGER, BERLIN/KARLSRUHE

Justice Ginsburg's exercise routine, the trainer she shares with other judges in the Capitol, and her ability to do 20 push-ups — in plank position, no knees! When reporter Jeffrey Toobin published an article referring to the Justice as "frail," Marty confronted him at a cocktail party, asking how many push-ups he could do in comparison. Toobin's endearing atonement appears in the form of a jacket blurb, describing the book as the "biography of a bad-ass"!

We learn of the love between the Justice and Marty, and we can read in his handwriting the winking sweet words he wrote to her shortly before he passed away. "You are the only person I have loved in my life, setting aside, a bit, parents and kids and their kids ..." and if you want to read the rest, you'll have to pick up a copy of the book. Suggesting that their relationship is a model that others might consider, the book contains a wonderful *American Gothic*–style photographic portrait of Marty Ginsburg, bare-legged, with an apron and dish cloth, side-by-side with his favorite Justice, hair pulled back, in a formal black judicial robe and bright white collar that perfectly offsets Marty's dish cloth.

But most important, we learn of the approach to the law that she learned from the civil rights movement, and that she practiced in working at the ACLU to end gender discrimination. These experiences have guided her career. Her strategy was to effect lasting change by increments and through patient staging, to put the legal building blocks in place to support social change, bit by bit, so the result would be both lasting and acceptable to the public as fair and good.

First, start with challenges to governmental regulations or statutes that are obviously based on nothing more than stereotypes, and that hurt men as well as women.

One of her favorite cases at the ACLU was *Weinberger v. Wiesenfeld*, in which a stay-at-home father whose wife had passed away challenged the Social Security rule that gave special benefits to mothers but not fathers. The Court agreed with RBG, who later described it as

> part of an evolution toward a policy of neutrality — a policy that will accommodate traditional patterns, but at the same time, one that requires removal of artificial constraints so that men and women willing to explore their full potential as humans may create new traditions by their actions.

RBG's approach (notorious or not) was about more than clever strategic thinking — to focus on harms to men, for example — but was part of a deep conviction that rigid gender stereotypes harm men as well as women, and that we all benefit from having an equal chance.

Another aspect of this work was to focus on reproductive freedom. In RBG's hopes, the Court would come to recognize pregnancy discrimination as a type of gender discrimination since only women can become pregnant. And the cases would develop first from challenges to governmental or corporate rules that required women to stop working upon becoming pregnant. Such cases provided a sympathetic starting point and base from which to build recognition of the way reproductive choice was critically tied to gender equality. In the Justice's ideal, the state reforms on abortion regulation would have been allowed to develop in the political sphere before the Supreme Court took up the specific question of constitutional protection for abortion rights, and the right itself would have been grounded in doctrines concerning equality more than privacy.

Whether this incremental and equality-based approach would have left us with the same or greater protections for reproductive choice than we have today is hard to know. Others had less patience, and the law developed along different lines.

The Supreme Court in 1973 was differently composed than it is now. *Roe v. Wade* adopted transformative protection for abortion rights, which had the effect of invalidating many state laws around the country, and has been a source of controversy ever since. While the Court in 1992 upheld the central right of a woman to be protected against "undue burdens" on the right to abortion, states continue to restrict abortion rights, with a goal of making the procedure inaccessible as a practical matter, especially for women without financial resources. A case from Texas that the Court will decide this term again puts the matter up for debate.

One of the themes of *Notorious RBG* and of the Justice's work has been about the importance of not being the only woman in the room, "something strange and singular," as she put it. Whether the presence of three women justices on the Court will matter to the disposition of the case from Texas is something we may never know, but the Notorious RBG Tumblr, I expect, will have something to say about it.

When you try to mix pop culture biography with legal theory, some areas are bound to miss the mark. You might wind up slapping a section on raising children in New York in the middle of an explanation of the judicial appointment process. Or you might include perhaps too much annotated material from briefs and opinions.

Why quibble though, when the book succeeds so mightily at its main purpose: providing a loving and energetic tribute to a justice who has tirelessly fought for equality and who has been a credit to the Supreme Court and to the law. It is both trumpet call and translation, presenting and interpreting RBG's work for a new generation that is waiting to take up the mantle and finish the job.

ORIGINALLY PUBLISHED ON JANUARY 30, 2016

SPHINX POEM

FADY JOUDAH

The magnolia had barely looped ten orbits
around the sun when we moved in. No Deep South
magnolia this Texas one. In Atlanta

an ancient magnolia stood at the center of a hospital
as if healing depended on it.
The poison, biohazard waste, blood at the roots.

If the windows were open
you could reach out, run
your pads over its wax without your tiptoes
calling on your cerebellum to intervene.

And when in bloom
the tree put on its Milky Way citrus bouquet
that had survived the extinction
dinosaurs couldn't. To exist

before bees did, to befriend
the primeval beetle and withstand
the weight of the gauche insect

with sheathed wings, the tree offered giant
armored flowers. ("Sheathed wings," *elytra*, Minecraft,
the sandbox that kidnaps children
and eats them.) Years later

after routine vampiric check up in clinic, our friends
who lived in the historic district and had a historic
magnolia percuss their windows on the second floor

found out their son had mild lead toxicity.
Historic pipes moved them
out. We lost

our visitation rights with the great Talauma. In 1703
while in Martinique, Charles Plumier
renamed the magnolia tree after his countryman
Pierre Magnol, the father

of modern botanic classification.
Then another father, nomenclatorial whiz
Carl Linnaeus honored Charles

by renaming a tree Plumeria.
The Frangipani, powerful
Roman family that gave of its own bread

to the people during a famine, and later stood behind
a Pope's investiture, also extracted perfume
from the flower, and possibly gave us Dante.

All around the world the frangipani goes by other names.
The Champa, The Egg Yolk
fools its moth, the sphinx moth, the humming bird

and hawkmoth (a Nabokov favorite).
Melia's bloom is nectarless. Its intense fragrance
inebriates the sphinx into pollinating it

with a proboscis gone fly fishing.
The tree thinks the high a fair trade
and the moth goes away hungry.

LOVE

KARL HAENDEL, *DEBBIE DOES MATH GROUP: HAND ON HEAD #2*, 2013, TARPAPER, PENCIL ON CUT PAPER, 45.5 X 45.5 X 2 INCHES FRAMED / COURTESY OF THE ARTIST, SUSANNE VIELMETTER LOS ANGELES PROJECTS, AND MITCHELL-INNES & NASH, NY / PHOTO: ROBERT WEDEMEYER

IV.

FREE SPEECH

AMERICAN SMUT: FREE SPEECH AND THE RIGHT TO MAKE A BUCK

JONATHAN SHAPIRO

HERE IS A HANDY PRIMER on the difference between art and film. Art involves the universal, timeless human need to express ideas and emotions. Film exists to make money. This is why it is called the film *industry*. Its products are manufactured in quantity through use of formulas for mass consumption. It isn't show *fun*. It is show *business*. To quote the cliché: When they say it's not about the money, what they mean is, it's about the money.

Like all company towns, Hollywood takes a wry view of the source of its wealth. Folks in Detroit make cracks about the car industry. People in Hollywood always took MGM's motto — "Ars Gratia Artis" — as an inside joke. Even today, contracts for above-the-line talent refer to the writers, actors, and directors as "*artists*." Whenever these contracts arrive in the mail, inevitably years after my services have been rendered or are no longer needed, I can almost hear the snickering of the in-house attorney who sent them, his homuncular tongue firmly in his pale, mottled cheek. They can call it the "Motion Picture *Academy*" — they can describe Vivid or other porn houses, or Paramount or Sony, as *studios*. It doesn't make them any more respectable than calling Supercuts a hair *salon*. Over the last 16 years, I've sat through enough story and production meetings to know for certain that nobody out here is looking to invest in art.

Like show business, Jerry Geltzer's *Dirty Words and Filthy Pictures: Film and the First Amendment* sounds sexier than it is. I mean that as a compliment. The most important part of any script is the title. Whatever you can promote on the poster, whatever sells the most tickets, *that's* what makes a hit. But Geltzer's book also delivers the goods. His one-volume history of efforts to control the content of American film is informative, engaging, and entertaining.

More importantly, it is a bracing reminder that, for most of its history, film was treated by the law as commerce, not art, and the First Amendment had nothing to do with it. Both film and art might have been better off when this was the case.

At the heart of the book are questions that have long dogged art and film: "Can ogling a forbidden image sow the seeds of rebellion? Can a curse word be an act of defiance? Should there be *any* limit to creative expression on film?"

The answers to these questions seem clear enough to me — no — but others are equally certain I am wrong. It has always been so. "While movies provided cost-effective entertainment for the masses and a massive economic boom for well-positioned investors, the projected image came under fire almost immediately."

In 1896, Edison Manufacturing Company's 18-second featurette, *The Kiss*, a reenactment of a scene from a stage play where a man and woman lip-lock, prompted one reviewer to fulminate: "The spectacle of the prolonged pasturing on each other's lips was hard to bear. When only life size, it was pronouncedly beastly. Magnified to Gargantuan proportions and repeated three times over it is absolutely disgusting."

From 1907 on, every American city of any size had its censorship boards enacting civil ordinances banning the showing of specific films, sometimes even whole genres. The criteria was, to put it nicely, subjective: "It's just our own opinion," one censor admitted. But that opinion reflected the prejudices of the day. They always do. Films of prizefights, including reenactments of past brawls, became the first popular genre. After African-American champ Jack Johnson took the title, Congress prohibited the sale of boxing films over state lines. In *Weber v. Freed*, a unanimous Supreme Court upheld the ban.

As Geltzer points out, not all the censors were bigots or prudes. Some were simply absurd. Chicago's chief film censor was Major Metellus Lucullus Cicero Funkhouser, who admitted his "methodology was based on personal taste," and who boasted:

> We have cut a good many miles of films — scene obscene, scenes of the nude, scenes of ugly violence, scenes reflecting on constituted authority — because we thought they were unsuitable to present before audiences, 80 per cent of whom are women and children.

Hell is paved with good intentions. As Geltzer points out, the censors often meant well. They were neither all enemies of culture nor unintelligent buffoons. Most were volunteers in a fight against forces they believed threatened their families, communities, and ways of life. The author's empathy is a reminder that free speech advocates and civil libertarians will fight for almost any form of expression, except the form that seeks to set standards or encourage personal responsibility over what is expressed.

But that doesn't make the act of censorship any less egregious. Geltzer doesn't mention him, but no Los Angeles–based journal should talk about censorship without paying homage to our homegrown champion of free speech, Carey McWilliams. The 20th century's first great chronicler of Southern California culture understood Hollywood's power to influence the nation and the world. As a liberal champion of the First Amendment, he stood foursquare against any effort to censor its products. His reasons had less to do with the people doing the censoring than with the idea of censorship itself.

"Whatever the individual motives of the censors may be, censorship is a form of social control," McWilliams wrote. "It is a means of holding a society together, of arresting the flux which censors fear. And since the fear cannot be appeased, the demands for censorship mount in volume and intensity. And one form of censorship can easily lead to other forms."

Of the many crimes of the censor, none is quite so sad as those visited upon Robert Goldstein. The son of a German Jew, he opened a costume shop that provided the costumes for D. W. Griffith's *The Birth of A Nation*. Geltzer writes dryly: "Inspired by Griffith's historic success and massive profits, Goldstein decided to produce his own movie." The triumph of profit over art — let alone good taste — is as old as Hollywood itself. Griffith had already done the Civil War, so Goldstein chose the Revolutionary War as his subject.

We will never know if his *The Spirit of '76* was any good, the film is lost, but the evidence is not encouraging. It contained, for example, the intriguing scene of "King George III crashing his fist in the face of kindly old Benjamin Franklin."

All we know for sure is Goldstein had lousy timing. Released in 1917, the film was banned as an affront to the United States's war ally Britain, "tantamount to treason," the Supreme Court holding that "the constitutional guaranty of free speech carries with it no right to subvert the purposes and destiny of the nation." Poor Goldstein was imprisoned under the Espionage Act and served three years. By the time he was released, his money was gone and his film destroyed. Goldstein eventually had to return to his father's homeland, where he "almost certainly died in the Holocaust." Who says Hollywood isn't a tough town?

For the first three decades of the film industry's existence, American "courts were not yet ready to consider motions pictures as speech worthy of constitutional protection." And local and state governments were not ready to give up censorship as a form of good government. "In addition to the moral uplift, the logistics of film regulation were attractive. Regulation was a revenue generator; boards charged distributors for examination and approval and charged theaters for permitted exhibitions."

Like other industries eager to avoid regulation, the film industry's response to censorship was self-regulation, creating its own commissions to ensure its products were clean and pure. By 1915, "the movie business had exploded to become the fifth largest industry in the nation, with capital investments topping $500 million." To preserve their business, Griffith, Adolph Zukor, and others created the National Association of the Motion Picture Industry to fight federal efforts to censor films. They developed a "Thirteen Points," listing things filmmakers would voluntarily refuse to show, including "prolonged demonstrations of passionate love," "depreciation of law officers," and "vulgar and improper gestures."

Self-censorship worked, but only up to a point. When courts did weigh in on the issue of government censorship, the industry invariably lost. In the *Mutual Film Corp. v. Industrial Commission of Ohio*, a unanimous Supreme Court upheld regulations under the Commerce Clause of the Constitution, "comparing the medium to a circus sideshow, long subject to restrictions on exhibition." Film was not free speech or art. The Court "reduced motion pictures to 'a business, pure and simple,'" one which had "a capacity for evil" that should be regulated to protect the impressionable.

This wasn't all bad for business. There was a lucrative trade in luridly advertised film that just passed muster as well as the outright underground porn. Like Prohibition, censorship increased demand for the illicit. Howard Hughes's *The Outlaw*triggered a legal wrangle that boosted ticket sales. Exploitation moguls like Kroger Babb made money with titles such as *Child Bride*, *She Shoulda Said 'No!'*, and *Mom and Dad*, where screenings were segregated by gender, and a "sexologist" gave lectures between shows. Russ Meyer was far from the first of his kind. Roger Corman and Samuel Z. Arkoff found gold skirting censorship laws with films that would become part of mainstream teen, taboo, and porn genres.

Change came in the early 1950s. In a case involving Roberto Rossellini's *The Miracle*, the Supreme Court finally "brought the medium of motion pictures under the protection of the First Amendment." Neither sacrilege nor the fact Rossellini had an affair and love-child with Ingrid Bergman justified banning the film.

And yet for years after, American film censorship kept a wide array of material from the public, including foreign films, films about social issues ranging from segregation to birth control, and films made by actors or directors deemed subversive in their personal lives. Geltzer does a nice job describing the long slog of cases that led the Supreme Court to redefine its view of obscenity and extend full First Amendment protection to film. As to whether the world is better off for being able to view *Deep Throat*or *Mona the Virgin Nymph*, the author is too polite to say.

After Geltzer's fine book, I read Melvyn Bragg's *The Book of Books*, a history of the King James version of the Bible. Perhaps I needed a moral palette cleaning. As Bragg notes, Protestantism, coupled with technological developments in printing, eventually ended what amounted to a thousand-year practical ban on the Bible. But the results only confirmed the censors' worst fears. The Bible turned out to be as inflammatory as feared, justifying all sorts of excess, not to mention revolution, regicide, and equal rights. It is possible that censors have a point — that free speech doesn't necessarily always serve the commonwealth's best interests. But try to explain that to a YouPorn viewer.

There is no reason to think the battle between free expression and government efforts to protect the governed will become less brutal in the future. If anything, the stakes have gotten higher. As Geltzer notes, "[s]ince 2004 more filmmakers have been investigated, tried, and convicted for the content of their films than in the fifty years prior."

As long as there's money to be made, the film industry will figure out some way to provoke and profit. The law gives them the right to show every manner of mortification, gratification, amorality, cruelty, and violence. It also affords prosecutors, rather than censors, the power to prosecute those who go too far. What "too far" means depends on public taste. We may not all agree as to what's obscene, but we all think we know it when we see it. If that isn't the definition of a meaningless, subjective, useless standard of law, I don't know what is.

ORIGINALLY PUBLISHED ON APRIL 30, 2016

SETH ALVERSON, *PRISON BUS*, 2014, OIL ON CANVAS, 24 X 55 INCHES

FREE SPEECH IN THE POST-GUTENBERG WORLD

STEPHEN ROHDE

THE EXPANSION of worldwide means of communications has been unprecedented. On October 29, 1969, the very first message was sent from a computer at the University of California, Los Angeles, to the Stanford Research Institute. A December 1969 map of what would eventually become the internet showed a total of four computers. In August 1981, there were just 213 internet hosts. The first-ever website was created in 1991.

As of 2015, there are approximately three billion internet users. There are about two billion smartphones across the world, which is projected to reach four billion by 2020. It is estimated that it would take about six million years to watch all the videos crossing global networks in a single month. Were each Facebook user counted as an inhabitant, Facebook would have a larger population than China.

In 1962, the media guru Marshall McLuhan predicted such developments in his visionary book *The Gutenberg Galaxy*, writing that "the new electronic interdependence recreates the world in the image of a global village." Timothy Garton Ash, a professor at the University of Oxford and the Hoover Institution at Stanford University, credits McLuhan in his latest book *Free Speech: Ten Principles for a Connected World* for his "extraordinary seerlike insight." But instead of the phrase "global village" — which he finds too small, homogeneous, and conformist — Garton Ash prefers the term "cosmopolis," which embraces "the entirety of this mixed-up, connected world-as-city" that exists in "the interconnected physical and virtual worlds."

The author of nine previous books, a regular contributor to *The New York Review of Books*, and a recipient of the George Orwell Prize, Garton Ash opens his intriguing new work with the sentence "We are all neighbours now." What concerns this British writer is how everyone in the cosmopolis can get along when it comes to the complicated issue of free speech. He recognizes that we live in a world of conflict and differences, which should not be made sterile, monotonous, uncreative, and unfree, and contends that "the way to live together well in this world-as-city is to have more and better free speech." His goal, in short, is to work out "a framework of civilised and peaceful conflict, suited to and sustainable in this world of neighbours." In doing so, Garton Ash offers a sweeping and sober conception of free expression, without naïveté or platitudes.

¤

The problem, according to Garton Ash, is that "[u]nnoticed by many of us, a great power struggle over the shape, terms, and limits of global freedom of expression is raging around us, inside that box in your pocket and perhaps even inside our heads." He calls it "word power," which includes "images, sounds, symbols, information, and knowledge, as well as structures and networks of communications." In the 21st century, previously open, free-wheeling technologies of communications are being reined in and constrained by both public and private powers. Indeed, the "internal, sometimes secret, operational practices of private superpowers may be more influential than the decisions of lawmakers and regulators." This is no longer "just a matter of a single national government telling you what you may or may not publish or broadcast in one country, or a single newspaper proprietor deciding what it will or will not print — the classic territory of twentieth-century literature on free speech."

Given the new interconnected cosmopolis, the fundamental challenge is whether the standards of free expression and the open exchange of information worldwide will rise to the level of the American First Amendment model, which Garton Ash considers "the most systematically pro-free speech jurisdiction in the world," or succumb to the Orwellian model in which an ominous combination of governmental censorship and private regulations stifles free speech and suppress information.

For a cautionary glimpse at what the Orwellian model actually looks like, Garton Ash describes the existing Chinese party-state, which claims the right to control all expression within its frontiers on the grounds of "maintaining cyberspace sovereignty." To be sure, the Chinese Constitution in Article 35 pays lip service to the principle that "citizens of the People's Republic of China enjoy freedom of speech, of the press, of assembly, of association, of procession, and of demonstration." In reality, however, a 2010 white paper from the Information Office of China's State Council chillingly declared that:

> no organisation or individual may produce, duplicate, announce or disseminate information having the following contents: being against the cardinal principles set forth in the Constitution; endangering state security, divulging state secrets, subverting state power and jeopardizing national unification; damaging state honour and interests; instigating ethnic hatred or discrimination and jeopardizing ethnic unity; jeopardizing state religious policy, propagating heretical or superstitious ideas; spreading rumours, disrupting social order and stability; disseminating obscenity, pornography, gambling, violence, brutality and terror or abetting crime; humiliating or slandering others, trespassing on the lawful rights and interests of others; and other contents forbidden by laws and administrative regulations.

China has constructed an elaborate public/private infrastructure that blocks, filters, and directs all internet traffic through "a vast, multi-agency bureaucracy of censorship and propaganda," which a major Harvard University study called "unprecedented in recorded world history." In 2011, an extraordinary 13 percent of social media was censored. Estimates of the number of employees in the various agencies of internet control range from 20,000

© GIL GARCETTI, *IRON: 16*

to 50,000. A 2013 internal Party document contemptuously exhorted party members to beware of seven dangerous concepts, including "promoting the West's idea of journalism, challenging China's principle that the media and publishing system should be subject to Party discipline" and "promoting 'universal values' in an attempt to weaken the theoretical foundations of the Party's leadership."

But, before the rest of us get too smug, much of Garton Ash's book also raises serious questions over how free speech is treated — mistreated — in Western democracies. Every society — including every democratic society — engages in censorship. For example, justified by "national security," the Obama administration has prosecuted more whistle-blowers under the 1917 Espionage Act than all former US presidents *combined*, and is threatening to add NSA whistle-blower Edward Snowden to that ignominious roster.

Garton Ash also looks beyond the United States to further examine limitations on free expression outside of authoritarian regimes. Article 19 of the 1966 International Covenant on Civil and Political Rights boldly declares: "Everyone shall have the right to freedom of expression," which includes "freedom to seek, receive and impart information and ideas of all kinds." However, this broad declaration is subject to several explicit limitations "such as are provided by law and necessary: (a) for respect of the rights or reputations of others; (b) For protection of national security or of public order (*ordre public*), or of public health or morals." In addition, Article 20 contains a mandate that "any propaganda for war" and "any advocacy of national, racial, or religious hatred that constitutes incitement to discrimination, hostility, or violence" shall be "prohibited by law."

The protection for freedom of expression in Article 10 of the European Convention on Human Rights adds further restrictions in the interests of "territorial integrity," "the prevention of disorder or crime," and "maintaining the authority and impartiality of the judiciary."

Article 4 of the International Convention on the Elimination of All Forms of Racial Discrimination adopted in 1965 requires that States Parties condemn "all propaganda and all organizations which are based on ideas or theories of superiority of one race or group of persons of one colour or ethnic origin, or which attempt to justify or promote racial hatred and discrimination in any form." Condemnation of such ideas may be laudable but the Convention goes further and instructs states to make the dissemination of those ideas "punishable by law," which several countries have done through the adoption and enforcement of hate speech laws.

Garton Ash argues that in mature democracies, which have the rule of law, diverse media, and a developed civil society, "the advantages of hate speech laws, as they have actually worked over the last half century, are outweighed by the disadvantages, including their unintended consequences." He supports his case with several disturbing examples.

In France, for example, there have been an annual average of 100 convictions per year between 1997 to 2001, which increased to 208 per year between 2005 to 2007. Actress Brigitte Bardot has been convicted five times for incitement to racial hatred for her fulminating attacks on Muslims starting with the way they slaughter animals. Distinguished intellectual Edgar Morin was found guilty for a fierce attack on Israel's treatment of Palestinians, and a member of parliament, Christian Vanneste, guilty for expressing "homophobic views," although both convictions were eventually overturned on appeals.

Garton Ash reveals the highly subjective double standards that are often at play when it comes to punishing hate speech. In 2006, the then secretary general of the Muslim Council of Britain, Sir Iqbal Sacranie (who once said death was perhaps too good for Salman Rushdie, against whom a fatwa had been declared for publishing *The Satanic Verses*) denounced the publication of the Danish cartoons depicting Muhammad, but scarcely a month later publicly declared that gays are "harmful" and "spread disease." Abraham Foxman and Christopher Wolf of the Anti-Defamation League argue that YouTube was right to leave up the controversial "The Innocence of Muslims" video but insisted that Facebook should take down Holocaust denials because they are hate speech.

To be sure, there are hopeful signs of movement toward a more free and open system. For instance, Garton Ash describes the 2009 decision of the Canadian Human Rights Tribunal holding that section 13 of the Human Rights Act, which mandates controls over hate speech on the internet, violated the free speech protections in Canada's Charter of Rights and Freedoms. The central contention of this book "is that we should limit free speech as little as possible by law and the executive action of governments or corporations, but do correspondingly more to develop shared norms and practices that enable us to make best use of this essential freedom."

¤

After spending nine months writing a book on free speech in the 20th century, Garton Ash asked himself: "If your subject is the post-Gutenberg world, how can you rest content with writing about it only in the old Gutenberg way?" Consequently, with a team at Oxford University, he developed an experimental website called freespeechdebate.com, which presents case studies, video interviews, analyses, and personal commentaries from around the world, much of it translated into 13 languages. (Since *LARB* is a post-Gutenberg online book review, readers can take a break and click on the Garton Ash's website, before returning to this book review).

Garton Ash traveled from Cairo to Berlin, Beijing to Delhi, New York to Yangon, and talked and listened about free speech. That experience informed and transformed the book, leading him to reorganize it around 10 Principles. His first principle, entitled "Lifeblood," expresses his fundamental concept: "We — all human beings — must be free and able to express ourselves, and to seek, receive, and import information and ideas, regardless of frontiers." We can trace this principle to the core of Article 19 of the 1966 International Covenant on Civil and Political Rights. Garton Ash explains why this is the First Principle: "Freedom of expression is not merely one among many freedoms. It is the one upon which all others depend."

The use of the term "human beings" is not mere rhetoric. For Garton Ash, "We" means "all the people," and should *not* be enjoyed by corporations. In the United States, "the most explicitly, and consistently pro-free speech country in the world, money howls through political campaigns." In the land of the First Amendment, "the limiting, distorting, and corrupting power of money is the biggest single cause for concern around free speech.

Money speaks, too loudly."

The rest of the 10 Principles focus on the most contentious free speech issues in the world today. How do we deal with dangerous speech that promotes violence? Can free speech be uncensored but subject to limitations? Should we enforce civility by law? Does shocking or offensive art and humor get a free pass? Does respect for religion require laws prohibiting speech that attacks religion? Can we protect individual privacy and personal reputations but ensure public scrutiny of matters of public interest? Is national security helped or hurt by protecting whistle-blowers and leakers? How do we maintain free speech on the internet, which is largely in the hands of private companies unbound by the First Amendment?

In clear and engaging prose, filled with scores of interesting examples and grounded in timely and comprehensive research, Garton Ash addresses all of these questions and more from a broad international perspective. For readers used to examining freedom of expression purely within the confines of the largely self-congratulatory American experience this book raises challenging issues in the context of a wide range of other countries and traditions.

A chapter entitled "Courage" features the 10th Principle: "We decide for ourselves and face the consequences." In keeping with his international approach, after citing icons of the Western tradition including Pericles, John Lilburne, John Milton, John Stuart Mill, and Justice Louis Brandeis, Garton Ash adds the story of a modern hero of free speech, Chinese dissenter Liu Xiaobo, who was sentenced to 11 years imprisonment in 2009 for "subverting state power." In his closing remarks to the court, Liu declared that he looked forward to the day "when our country will be a land of free expression: a country where the words of each citizen will get equal respect, a country where different values, ideas, beliefs, and political views can compete with one another even as they peacefully coexist." Underscoring the impact of Liu's remarks, the judge cut him off before he could finish. What he had written, and would have said, was that "I hope that I will be the last victim in China's long record of treating words as crimes. Free expression is the base of human rights, the root of human nature, and the mother of truth. To kill free speech is to insult human rights, to stifle human nature, and to suppress truth."

Garton Ash ends by calling for "realistic idealism and idealistic realism." His impressive book is a testament to his belief that the "[o]ngoing debate about the limits to and positive conditions for free speech is itself a vital ingredient of free speech." The challenge Garton Ash presents is important. But the outcome of this vital debate does not rest only in the hands of brilliant observers like Garton Ash. It is our shared responsibility. The question he leaves us with is, are we up to the task?

ORIGINALLY PUBLISHED ON NOVEMBER 16, 2016

KARL HAENDEL, *RODEO 10*, 2016, PENCIL AND GRAPHITE POWDER ON PAPER, 103 X 83 INCHES / COURTESY OF THE ARTIST, SUSANNE VIELMETTER LOS ANGELES PROJECTS, AND MITCHELL-INNES & NASH, NY / PHOTO: JEFF MCLANE

AT PRITCHESS DETENTION CENTER

SUSANNAH NEVISON

The Active Denial System uses electromagnetic radiation to stun targets with heat. In 2010, Pritchess Detention Center sought to install it.

It's no different than the game
we played as children: a dry leaf,
a magnifying glass to focus
the sun's ray, a little smoke
for show, to show the others
how the thing gets done. The leaf
never amounts to the fire
you would hope, but master
the basics and what you flame next
depends on what's at hand: a twig
or two, a piece of paper, a line of ants.
From a distance, you'll need
a steady grip, a real keen eye,
great aim. Once they feel
the heat, it's only a matter
of time until they flee. How
a thing gets done: you set them
running right into God's arms,
and then you set them free.

CELL WATCH: STRIP CELL

SUSANNAH NEVISON

Consider the cell not as you see it
but as it comes to be: a world
unto itself, the garden, uncharted
and rife with wildness, beasts unnamed.
One man to one small room—you
grant him dominion so that he might
render the room expansive and rich,
his kingdom, stretch his mind
indefinitely. But since this is the beginning
of the world, it's up to you
to define the edges, contour
the known, to introduce the common
language: show him how this world
is nothing more than God's hand
grenade spinning through the air.
From the burning, you won't save him.
You'll build a room within a room,
another world to hold what's left
of this one. A box, rough pomegranate
wood, inlaid. Inside, a body's rough
material, a gift to God, a rib.

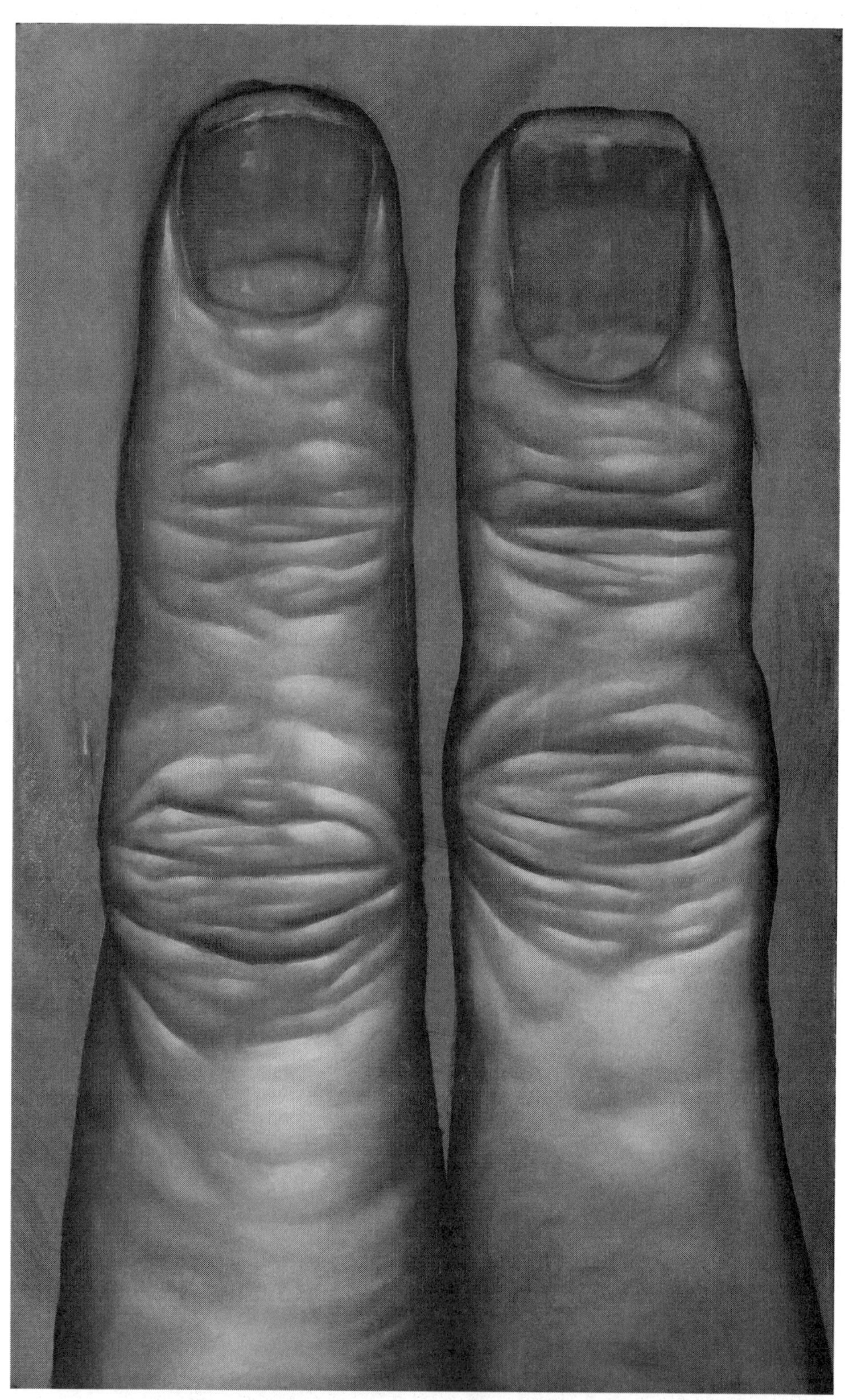

SETH ALVERSON, *FINGERS*, 2013, OIL ON CANVAS, 29 X 18 INCHES

V.

HUMAN RIGHTS

—

AN EXTRAORDINARY PERSON

AMEENA MIRZA QAZI

"THE TRUTH IS, anyone can be turned," I recently explained to family members as we sat around my parents' living room, discussing whether a new acquaintance was a government informant — a person invading our personal and religious spaces to pass on information to the US government. "Everyone has something to lose, or to gain, and if the right pressure points are pressed, they will turn. It takes an extraordinary person to withstand that kind of pressure."

An extraordinary person. And this is in the American context, where we can debate such issues to the drone of Fourth of July fireworks and not precision drone strikes; where disappearances and arbitrary detentions are *so* 2002. What does resistance now look like under an extremely suppressive and violent regime? How much easier would it be to pressure activists to abdicate their struggles? Looking at the life of Shirin Ebadi, the answer is: Not easy at all. Ebadi is a lawyer, human rights activist, and former Irani judge, who won the Nobel Peace Prize in 2003 for her human rights work in Iran. Her latest autobiographical work, *Until We Are Free*, describes her struggle to erect the rule of human rights law in Iran after winning the Nobel Peace Prize.

Ebadi quickly debunks the notion that the life of a Nobel laureate is one in which the doors of progress open widely and tyranny abates under the world's watchful eye with the prestige of the Nobel Prize serving as unassailable armor. Instead, as the Ahmadinejad reign devolves into further paranoiac policies and human rights violations abound — arbitrary detentions, the brutal suppression of political protests, the denial of access to attorneys, sham criminal charges like "conspiracy against national security" and the "dissemination of lies" — Ebadi and her colleagues are only further persecuted, putting their life and liberty on the line to salvage the remnants of Irani freedom.

It is not easy to divine the truth of human rights struggles in the context of culture wars between "East" and "West." I have become fatigued with self-made and self-congratulatory stories of struggle, in which to acquire aspects of Western privilege, the writer has to discard her culture, heritage, and religion — effectively reinforcing false cultural binaries and the exclusivity of first-world liberalism.

In contrast, I felt with Ebadi's writing something I so often fail to have — trust. She describes from the outset how she used the tenets of Islam to argue the case for human and women's rights in Iran's judicial system. Her writing is rife with simple depictions of Irani life — I felt like I was walking the streets of Iran with her, sharing her food, comforting her clients as she offers them tea. She sets the stage of the movement firmly in Irani soil so that the reader *knows* that freedom, human decency, liberation, and honor, are concepts intrinsic to Iran. Like breathing the smog-filled air over Tehran that she describes, the reader cannot help but be saturated with how natural and vital to the Irani people the struggle for freedom is.

At the same time, Ebadi expertly encourages the reader to generalize from the lessons of her struggle, and to relate it to the global struggle for human rights. The clearest way she does this is with the Nobel Women's Initiative, which she created with other Nobel laureates to advance global peace with justice and equality. But, interestingly, the way that I most connected with Ebadi's writing was not as a Muslim or a woman, but as an attorney committed to the rule of law. This commitment is repeated throughout Ebadi's narrative, even when she is wary of any actual legal recourse; she is indefatigable in pursuing justice for her clients. In describing her defense of Haleh Esfandiari, an Irani-American Middle East scholar arbitrarily arrested and prohibited from returning to DC's Woodrow Wilson International Center for Scholars, Ebadi writes:

> Often I felt as though I were rushing about in the darkness, banging on doors, searching for the elusive person who mattered, the individual who could reveal what was actually going on. [...] There wasn't much I could do, but as I certainly needed to do something, I gave interviews about the case to the press, often hourly.

Ebadi also avoids glamorizing the lives and choices of those resisting the degradation of Iran's legal system. I particularly appreciated her candor in describing difficult choices she faced throughout the years — including telling her secretary to "stand-down" during an office raid, deciding whether to board a plane that likely meant facing death or imprisonment, and learning to understand and cope with personal betrayal. People like to believe that the life of a revolutionary is black and white — that one either fights or capitulates. By genuinely reconstructing the nuances underlying her decisions, she helps empower other agents of change to embrace their own humanity in unpredictable and uphill struggles for justice.

At several points throughout the book, when Ebadi describes the ways her contemporaries suffer because of her activities, I felt like yelling at the pages, "It's not about you!" And it was not until nearly the end of the book that I realized that this was my own glamorization of a human rights lawyer's life. I had been assuming that support for what she does swells from the people surrounding her — first and foremost from the people she loves. But Ebadi's reality was starkly different: the persecution of her colleagues and family members was unambiguously due to the state's vendetta against her.

This illuminates the beautiful crux of Ebadi's book. *Until We Are Free* is a story as much about the voices of her clients as it is about her. After being removed from the bench after the 1979 revolution and becoming a human rights lawyer, Ebadi used whatever tools she had available to advance the causes of her clients. True to form, she is using her international prestige and amazing tale to call the world's attention to her contemporaries and amplify the voices of those who have been silenced — like Akbar Ganji, a reformist journalist who had lain forgotten and emaciated by a hunger strike in Evin Prison; or Mohammad Seifzadeh, Ebadi's co-counsel on a case representing Baha'is (a religious minority), injured under state sanctioned violence, and who has spent six years in prison for his activities; or Mehrangiz Kar and her husband Siamak Pourzand, both of whom spent time in prison for Kar's activities as a human rights lawyer, the latter of whom resolved his depression and illness (both contracted while in jail) by taking his life from the top of an apartment building.

It takes an extraordinary person to withstand state-sponsored brutality and personal setbacks, but it takes supernatural strength to maintain hope and faith when faced with these hurdles.

Ebadi shares with the reader — with deep humanity and earnest love for her homeland, faith, and rule of law — how she has achieved this supernatural feat, while crossing worlds of misunderstanding to show that the struggle for freedom shall never perish, and that in believing so, we too, can be extraordinary.

ORIGINALLY PUBLISHED ON AUGUST 17, 2016

ANNE LIBBY, *DIE, REGENERATE OR MULTIPLY (BENCHES BRANCH)*, 2015, HIGH-DENSITY POLYETHYLENE, POWDER COATED STEEL / COURTESY THE ARTIST AND NIGHT GALLERY / PHOTO: JEFF MCLANE

INHERITING INJUSTICE AND PERPETUATING IMPUNITY:

WHAT YOU DIDN'T KNOW ABOUT GUANTÁNAMO

ANNE RICHARDSON

Since this piece was published, in June of 2016, the landscape in the United States has changed dramatically. Instead of discussions about closing Guantánamo, there are now threats to expand it. The new administration has drafted, but as of the date of this update, not issued, an Executive Order that contemplates filling the base again with alleged ISIS fighters. So, while President Obama deserves credit for bringing the number of detainees down to 41 before leaving office, he was not able to rub out the prison's continuing existence as a place of indefinite detention beyond the rule of law. Remaining open, it is still available as a recruiting tool to our foes; a saber that can be rattled for those who seek to gain power through stirring up fear; and a reminder of our failure to live up to our American promise whose final chapter is not yet written.

¤

ON JANUARY 22, 2009, President Barack Obama signed his first executive order, promising to close Guantánamo Bay "no later than one year from today." As can be seen from the videotape of that signing ceremony, he was less than clear on what was going to actually happen to the detainees, asking "Greg," off camera, if there was a separate executive order regarding how they would be "disposing of the detainees." He was reminded in a vague response, that they would be "setting up a process."

Ah yes, "the process."

What must count among Obama's sharpest regrets is the way in which he mishandled his inheritance from George W. Bush. Just as *Thirteen Days*, the critically acclaimed history of Kennedy's handling of the Cuban Missile Crisis, presents a case study in how to handle an international crisis, *Obama's Guantánamo* presents a case study in missed opportunities.

Many may be tempted to attribute Obama's failure in closing the camp to conservatives who outflanked him — even Obama has made this claim. Indeed, they passed legislation that made his job harder, cried "terrorism," and sparked fear of transferring detainees. But *Obama's Guantánamo*, edited by Jonathan Hafetz of Seton Hall Law School, which presents 14 essays from lawyers who work behind the scenes in the civilian habeas bar and the military commissions, makes the case that Obama lost his way more than once when he had the chance to do the right thing, and retreated to the same failed positions of his predecessor.

Candidate Obama campaigned heavily on the basis that he would close Guantánamo and restore the United States's global leadership on the rule of law. Public opinion was so galvanized against the loss of constitutional rights that Guantánamo represented, that even candidate John McCain agreed before the election of 2008 that the detainee camp at Guantánamo Bay should be closed. At an estimated cost of $4 million per detainee per year, a majority of Americans agree with them both.

Yet as demonstrated by these personal essays from attorneys negotiating with the transition team and arguing with the administration's Justice Department, Obama did not make the clean break that he suggested he would. For example:

- Obama repeatedly signed rather than vetoed legislation that barred transfer of detainees to the United States, and which restricted the use of funds to transfer them to foreign countries;

- Obama revised rather than rejected the flawed military commissions system, continuing to argue, among other things, that even if detainees were found not guilty they could be detained indefinitely, there is no right to speedy trial, and hearsay is admissible;

- Obama's lawyers successfully argued in court, as the Bush administration had, that even when a Court ordered a detainee to be released, it could not force the Executive Branch to do so;

- Obama rejected calls to prosecute those who approved, committed, or permitted torture on detainees captured and kept in prisons in Afghanistan, Guantánamo, and black sites throughout the world, granting immunity to all participants in this historic injustice;

- Obama's lawyers successfully argued to dismiss cases against extraordinary rendition by raising the very same "state secrets" doctrine that was raised by the Bush administration;

- Obama's lawyers successfully argued that detainees imprisoned at Bagram Air Base in Afghanistan had no right to bring a claim of habeas corpus in the United States, even after the *Boumedienne*decision held that the detainees in Guantánamo Bay could do so.

Obama's Guantánamo's 14 essays range in style from the chatty first-person narrative to the sober assessment of policy. The attorneys range from corporate pro bono counsel to nonprofit attorneys and professors of law. (In full disclosure, this reviewer has represented a detainee since 2008.) Each provides an insight into a different facet of the maze that confronts those who agree to step into the representation of men held out as, but never proven to be, the "worst of the worst." Franz Kafka is invoked more than once as the only way to explain the nonsensical processes that are served up to these attorneys as their only path forward. Success or failure seems less the result of good lawyering — although there is much in evidence — than the politics behind the US relationship with the detainee's home countries. Yet the inside stories behind the headlines make for engrossing reading and will be an indispensable part of the public record of this phase in American history.

This book arrives just as President Obama has made a renewed push to clear and transfer as many men as possible before his term is up. From 242 men in Guantánamo Bay when he took office, to 122 men when some of the essays were written, we are now down to 80, and that number is shrinking monthly. With the knowledge that his term is indeed coming to an end, Obama has announced a new pledge to give more of the men an abbreviated hearing on whether they constitute a current threat to the United States and to transfer all those cleared, assuming the Department of Defense gives the green light. The hearings and transfers would leave only those charged with military crimes, or those deemed too dangerous to release but not capable of being tried, whom he would seek to transfer to the United States.

Whittling down the number of detainees held without trial in Guantánamo has undoubtedly been good policy. However, Obama's plan still includes a role for indefinite detention without trial, an idea that before Guantánamo was completely anathema to the United States legal system. It violates not only our Constitution, which the authorities attempted to sidestep by placing detainees in our naval station in Cuba, but also international law. Obama may have inherited injustice, for which we can all sympathize. But we cannot set back civilized society and the rule of law by tolerating any plans to perpetuate impunity. We must demand what our principles require: either provide them with fair trials, or let the men go.

ORIGINALLY PUBLISHED ON JUNE 7, 2016

GOOD SHARE

NATALIE SHAPERO

An airport — like a hog farm,
like a landfill, like a graveyard —

has to go somewhere. An airport
has to go somewhere, so
why not here? I nominate you

and you and me to roil
in our respective beds while planes

fly so low overhead we can tell
what makes they are. The yowl
of the Airbus, the Boeing's

Gregorian roar. At least they drown
out the rest of this inexcusably human

night: longneck bottle greeting
the side of a passing car,
strange chanting, fistfight too close

to the tracks, the neighbors
with their nonstop innovation

in the arena of sex offender registry
drinking games. View the mugshot,
guess the offense, drink a shot if

you're wrong. Eleven men in ten
locations: guess which two guys

split a duplex. Drink a shot
if you're wrong. Plug in the ocean
in order to find out if anyone's

currently in the ocean and if
we, consequently, should avoid it.

Do you think we should avoid it?
Drink a shot if you're
wrong. Drink while you can,

because I heard from a dead guy
there's no alcohol in Heaven.

I also heard no alcohol
on Earth. If you're drinking right
now, buddy, you're in Hell.

SANAZ KHOSRAVI, *FALSE ROOTS (FROM THE REVOLUTION IS NOT OVER SERIES)*, 2016

"WHAT ARE YOU DOING HERE, SISTER?"

LAMYA H

I.

IN THE BEGINNING, there was a plane; 22 hours in flight, and two layovers, and finally, finally, a slow descent.

The overhead lights flicker on. I wake up to the artificial morning of the aircraft: breakfast service and a line for the bathroom and the sounds of restless sleepers stirring. Open my window slowly to temper the sudden flood of sunlight, kiss the tip of my nose to warm plexiglass, and look down. For my first view of this city, this infamous city, this city that will become home.

This is a city I have loved from afar, its culture and chaos telecast across an ocean and written into books I have devoured. Bridges and tall buildings, a statue rising out of the sea. Neighborhoods with names exotic to my teenage tongue: the Upper West Side, SoHo, Flushing Meadows. Swatches of color outside my airplane window, the gray of roads and blue of ocean grow closer and closer until out of nowhere the tarmac comes into view and there is the familiar bump of wheels hitting ground. "Welcome to John F. Kennedy Airport," the pilot's voice booms, "We hope you fly with us again."

In the beginning, there was a plane and then, there was the airport. A border between me and the city, and guarding this border, a grim line of immigration booths.

I wait in the separate queue for foreigners, a long line that curls several times in its pen. Use this time to catch up to finally being stationary, my body still wading through viscous air, my ears still faintly humming. At my turn I step up to the booth and plaster on a smile, but I can immediately tell that the border agent does not appreciate the combination of my disorientation and my hijab and my brown skin. He flips to the shiny new student visa in my passport, and then looks down at me from his glass-enclosed dais. Pulls my eyes into full contact with his ice blue gaze and asks for the address where I'll be staying for the week before college starts. At my uncle's, I say, but I can't remember the house number, street, or suburban town; can barely remember my uncle's face from the last time I saw him.

There is a pause.

The border agent's eyes narrow and his mouth purses: he stares at me, waiting to see if I flinch. (I don't. But my stomach, always first to betray the physicality of my nervousness lets out a long, low growl.) He steps out of the booth and asks me to follow him. A left turn and an embarrassing walk down the row of people being more successfully questioned. I'm led into a sterile side room.

In the beginning, there was a plane and an airport, and then there was a white-tiled room. The infamous secondary questioning. With fluorescent lights and steely officers and large signs forbidding the use of cell phones. Hard plastic chairs, and in them, people of different shades of brown. Together, we sweat fear and feign nonchalance as we sit in an expectant silence, broken only by the butchered announcement of our names.

I wait. Not very long — but long enough to map out how I would face the embarrassment of being sent back; long enough for my insides to liquefy. I'm called up to the desk. There are two officers this time and they have more questions: What do I want to study? Why this university? Why this city? Where am I meeting my uncle? Do I have his phone number? Why am I traveling alone? Did anyone besides me pack my bags?

Eventually satisfied, they let me go. My suitcase has arrived before me at the carousel. I pick it up and wheel it through customs and the gate, and then finally, finally, I'm through. There is my uncle and he looks exactly like the hazy picture in my mind and he hugs me tight and hands me a giant bag of Doritos that he remembers me loving when I was eight years old. Never before have I been so happy to see someone I hardly know.

"Did you have any trouble at immigration?" he asks.

I muster up all the bravado of my 17 years of living. "Nah."

II.

I'm never homesick, never culture-shocked in this city. The contours are too familiar, too similar to the city I have left behind. The chain stores dotting the streets and the gray lights of office buildings. On humid days, on nights before trash days, on corners with throngs of people and halal food carts, it even smells like home.

Besides, I'm too busy teaching myself American. I learn to stretch out my vowels to sound like I'm from here. Replace my antiquated diction — thrice, fortnight, and so on — with short hard words that spit off my tongue and don't draw titters. Shed stiff button-down shirts for soft tees, easy two-piece hijabs for light printed department store scarves wound twice around my head and held with pins. I learn to blend into a thrilling anonymity.

I refuse to miss people and places. But after a while, I get tired of the food. Dining hall fare first, the pizza and pasta that are the standard unimaginative vegetarian default at every meal, then the creamy, oily curries that pass for South Asian fare at the restaurants nearby. Even Doritos I get tired of, when I overindulge on a giant bag of Cool Ranch after a day of missing all normal human meal time hours.

I find myself craving daal-chawal-bhindi. Not the rice that is the gloopy brown stuff in my dorm's dining hall, but chawal: individual basmati grains, fragrant and perfectly steamed. Okra I have barely seen, once in a while in a stew but mysteriously slimy and dull and tasteless, nothing like my mom's shallow-fried, crisp bhindi smothered in caramelized onions and buttery potatoes. Daal, I have almost forgotten the taste of.

I ask my mother for recipes. She emails me photos of elaborate instructions written out in her barely legible cursive. She's too slow at typing, she says, so these photos will have to do. Photos of her writing — half transliterated Urdu, half English, all love. I arm myself with this love.

Go to Jackson Heights, I am told, take the F train to the 74th Street–Roosevelt Avenue stop and walk around there and you'll find stores with what you need. I got this, I tell myself, how hard can this be?

It's my first journey out of Manhattan, my first solo trip on the subway. I ride the train with a practiced calm. Arrange my face into the blasé of someone who does this every day, sneak multiple checks at the sign on the platform that says Uptown/Queens, hide that I'm checking the map at every station we stop at to make sure I'm going the right way. I end up standing up out of my seat too early, right after the train pulls out of the station before. The F runs express in Queens and I sway holding the bar for long minutes until my stop.

Shahrukh Khan greets me as I step out of the station. His head, alongside some brand of fancy watch, both blown up to unnatural size. Store signs with scripts that I haven't seen in months. Tears in my eyes at the snatches of words floating in the air: inshallah, ayyo, rukh-ho, full throated letters that shove into my chest and settle somewhere between my heart and my stomach. The unmistakable odor of deep fried pakoras that seeps into my jacket, and suddenly I'm crying and I'm not sure if it's from the pop of my taste buds or because it'll be so hard to get rid of the smell.

I wander around a little. In the shade under the subway tracks, I pass uncles drinking chai, aunties choosing fruit and little kids riding tricycles. I duck into a relatively less crowded grocery store. The people inside take an extended look at my sloppy jeans and hesitation and immediately offer to help. Where are you from, beti? What town, what neighborhood, who are your people? When did you come here? How are you liking this city? They help me decipher the names of spices from my mother's recipes, translate from Urdu to English to visual, pick out the transparent sleeves of powders. I coo at a customer's baby. The woman restocking the shelves gives me imli candy. Offers opinions on snacks, on where to eat in the area, where to pray nearby now that I've spent so long in this store and sunset is approaching.

SETH ALVERSON, *PRISON WINDOW*, 2013, OIL ON CANVAS, 30 X 24 INCHES

I make my way to the winding line at the cash register. There's a panel of magazines alongside, and one catches my eye while I'm in line: a beautiful cover featuring some famous woman I half recognize, seductively turned toward the camera, eyes shiny and smiling, lips slightly parted. Probably an image that has caught my eye half a million times, and my body responds the way it always has: a slowly suffusing of warmth in my lower stomach, my eyes widening.

But something is different this time, maybe it's the dull ache of possibility. That I'm surrounded in school by women who identify with words that still feel strange on my tongue: lesbian, bisexual, queer. That my soccer teammates are dating each other openly, brazenly. That I'm beginning to recognize my feelings for women as desire, that I'm beginning to realize that these feelings have always been there and will never go away. That here, so far away from the people I know, I can invent myself anew.

When it's my turn to pay, I am suddenly shy. Can they see through me, these people who have been so helpful and kind? Can they tell from how long I lingered in front of the magazine? Would they be as loving if they knew? Come again, they say. Study hard, beta. Visit us soon.

I hand over what I owe and leave quickly, into the anonymity of the city.

III.

My brother comes to visit. It's a crisp November — my favorite weather, my favorite season in this city. Central Park alit with trees changing color, a bite to the air that's perfect for running. The occasional brief snowfall that covers the streets in white dust.

My brother comes to visit, and I decide to tell him I'm queer.

I'm starting to tell some friends here and there, but I've never bought into this idea of coming out. Have never thought I would tell someone who was related to me, never felt the need to, and besides there's the terrifying permanence of kinship. Once the words are said there is no going back with family, no cut and run.

In this case though, my decision to tell is strategic. My brother is coming to visit, and I want him to be able to talk to me. He's been having problems of his own: he has moved back home and things seem better, but it's hard to know what's going on because he won't talk to us. I want to support him as best as I can, my little brother whom I love, I love, but I need him to confide in me first, need him to see me as a complex person with issues of my own, and not just as his intimidating older sister — so I decide to tell him that I'm queer.

That's the easy part, the deciding. It's harder to figure out what to say: how much to reveal to my brother who, despite our closeness, I have never talked to about any romantic entanglements, his or mine. What words do I use? Queer, which feels more ambiguous, more true — or gay, which requires no explanation? And then, the fears: Will he ask questions I'm not ready to answer? Will he want justifications? Will he bring up Islam?

We're busy for the first few days after he arrives making lists, and doing touristy things, and meeting my friends, and there just isn't time to sit down and talk.

But then. I play hooky from work one day. I call it Sibling Day, and take my brother to Staten Island. Ferry ride, Sri Lankan food, distance from the everyday stuff of life: it's the perfect adventure.

We set off early — right after rush hour, when the subway is languid and exhales in the empty spaces left by panicked morning commuters. Park ourselves on the rear deck of the ferry for the best view of the city as the boat pulls away. The tip of the island, with tall blue buildings reflecting the water, the weak wintery sun. Wind on our faces and the wake of the boat in the water. The indulgence of a day off while the imaginary people in skyscraper windows work and work and work.

This feels like the perfect time. I lead the conversation to the night before when he had met a few of my close friends, almost all of them visibly queer. I ask him who his favorites are, and then.

"Did you like M?"

"Yeah, she's really great."

"Isn't she? I have a crush on her." I look out onto the water so that I don't have to face him.

He doesn't skip a beat.

"Oh really. That's cool. I also really liked F, she has great taste in music." Keeps talking and I'm not sure he's grasped what I'm trying to tell him, so I try again.

"I'm glad you like M. I have a really, really huge crush on her."

"Oh," he says, unflappable. "You should ask her out."

And then we talk about someone else, but I can hardly remember who or what, all I remember is shaking. Part involuntary response, part relief. I'm thankful to the rock of the boat for hiding my tremors.

We arrive in Staten Island soon after. Walk through cobbled lanes, snaking wide streets with rundown houses until we get to Dosa Garden. We eat and head back — we're early for the ferry so I take him on a detour. To Bay Street, at the tip of this island, where Eric Garner died, to the makeshift memorial of candles and photos and flowers.

Have you been here before, my brother asks, and I tell him I have. For a protest a few months ago, after a grand jury decided not to indict the police officer who killed Garner. Killed him as he pleaded *I can't breathe*, *I can't breathe*, 11 times over, *I can't breathe*. The anger, the despair of the crowds that day, the callousness of the police trying to control us in the interest of this city. Gray skies that threatened to break asunder and pour rain on us. My burgeoning consciousness and my tears and my rage. I tell my brother this at the spot

© GIL GARCETTI, *IRON: 117*

where I saw two kids at the protest, two brown kids, two angry kids, two rightfully angry kids get brutally arrested. I'm shaking again. I can't stop shaking.

On the ride back, we sit on a bench on the side of the ferry. It's my brother's turn to talk and he does. Tells me that though he's still worried about things, he is better. He talks. It's clear that he's being responsible, thoughtful, and I'm infinitely less worried. My plan has worked.

IV.

She insists that we rent a car to get to the wedding. It's not *that* far away, I argue, we can take the PATH to the hotel, maybe bum a free ride back to the city. But she is insistent, refuses to wear her finery on the train and is indignant about my brilliant plan to change in the bathroom at the station. It's either a car or a hotel room, she says, and the car ends up being cheaper, so car it is.

"What finery are you planning on wearing anyway?" I say when she shows up at my place with a duffel bag to do this thing women apparently do together called getting ready. We're going to our friend's wedding, the first of our friends to get married, my first brown wedding without the buffer of my parents to ensure that I'm following social code.

So, of course, I fuck up. I wear a kurta — masculine cut, and plain and the most comfortable of all the brown clothes I own. Dress it up with a silk hijab and wear a real bra even, but it's not until I get there that I realize that I am significantly under-dressed. Friends pull me aside all night to yell at me that my get up is not feminine enough.

But she. She knows exactly what she's doing, this white girl from Maine. Goes into my bedroom with her duffel bag and emerges wearing a black silk sari. Intricate gold designs all along the pallo, shimmering eye shadow and a dusting of gold glitter on her face. Long earrings that brush her neck when she moves, long hair that caresses the strip of soft skin between the bottom of her blouse and the top of her skirt. I can't tear my eyes away, and she smirks at my embarrassment.

She knows, she must know what she's doing to me, what she has been doing to me all month. At my first Dyke March, a few weeks before, she'd accompanied me — as an ally, she said to block photos, or for company in case I was overwhelmed and wanted to leave. She stepped out of the march to get me chocolate custard when we passed Shake Shack, and my friends asked if we were together. Some days later at a birthday party I had taken her to, where she didn't leave my side all night, where she kept whispering snarky comments in my ear and I couldn't stop giggling, friends asked if we were together.

All night, at this wedding, I can't tear my eyes away. She catches me staring while we're standing in line for dinner. Flashes a smile. Shimmies her shoulders at me, and my lips curl upward; we weave our own private cocoon in this pulsating party of 300 people. Later, when the groom's cousins put on an elaborately choreographed dance, she slips her hand into mine. Underneath the table, we hold hands. I have to remind myself to breathe.

I decide at that moment that I'm going to tell her I'm in love with her. This has gone on too long, I'm going to tell her, I'm going to do it tonight.

It's not like I haven't practiced what to say, I have. I've written it out. I've said it aloud to the mirror. I have it down pat. But it's hard to translate the words to movements of lips and tongue and air.

The words won't come out of my mouth, not when we're finally alone and collapsing into the car at the end of the night, not when she takes off her heels and hitches up her sari to settle into the driver's seat, not when she warbles along to the radio as she pulls out of the parking lot. I tell myself I'll do it when we reach the freeway. But by then we're too busy comparing notes on the food, on the people. Our conversation peters out and I tell myself I'll do it when this song is over. But then we're on the New Jersey turnpike, distracted by the city rising in front of us in all its Saturday night glory. Alit with the constellations of yellow bulbs in skyscrapers windows. The Lincoln Tunnel is my last chance. I promise myself I'll do it as soon as we're on the other side of the fluorescent monstrosity because who wants to be told they're loved under the dirty waters of the Hudson, under the harsh glow of endless fluorescent lights. But this is my last chance, I tell myself. I have to do it, I have to do it tonight.

"You look beautiful," I say. The words tumble out as soon as we emerge out of the tunnel, into the streets of the city.

She turns slightly to look at me, one eyebrow raised. "Thanks?"

"Really. You look beautiful. And, uh, I have to tell you something."

"Okay."

I do it. I tell her.

She is silent. Through a difficult left turn that makes her furrow her forehead and stick out her tongue in concentration, and then she is silent through a tense red light. Won't look at me while she recites the standard rejection. My ears buzz and I catch only phrases. *Thank you. I'm flattered. I appreciate our friendship*. Each one, a shard of glass, and then. The sentence — a death sentence — that I will remember for the rest of my life. *If you were a guy, things would be different.*

We reach my building. Park around the block, and I say, *that's cool.* I say the words that I've practiced too — the ones for the aftermath of her rejection. That I hope this doesn't change our friendship, that I just had to do this for myself. For a more honest friendship, I just needed to tell her, that's all. I'm eerily calm. She finally turns to look at me, and there's something unreadable in her eyes.

We get out of the car, she to grab her wallet from her bag in the back seat, me to leave, and she grabs my fingertips. Asks if she can hug me. Of course, I say. She pulls me close. Her hand reaches for my face, the backs of her fingers graze my cheek, her perfume — gardenias I think — curls around me. When I open my eyes, which I didn't even know were closed, her face is right next to mine. Her lips graze my jaw somewhere between my chin and my ear lobe. She kisses me.

On my cheek.

Drops her head to my shoulder and we hold each other. Standing on a street corner, enveloped by the anonymity that this city affords us, this dark Saturday night in this quiet neighborhood, we're just two girls, holding each other.

She pulls away after a while. "Thank you for telling me," she says. "See you at the dinner thing on Tuesday?"

"Yeah." I say as I get out of the car.

I smell the gardenias on me for days.

V.

I'm biking home from Brooklyn one beautiful spring night. Late enough on a Saturday that the city is still, dark streets aglow with the gold of streetlights and barely any cars. I whizz through red lights, even though I am in no hurry to get home.

It has been a wonderful night. "Queer Muslim Show and Tell," a brilliant idea by my friend, where we've all shared something we're passionate about. Things that we didn't know about each other: my friend who is a serious academic reads us the poetry that she writes in her free time; another friend brings a comic book collection to show us; another talks about the anti-violence project she's starting up at her mosque.

It has taken me a while to find these people, this group of queer Muslims who will spend a Saturday night sharing parts of themselves. It has taken me years dragging myself to lesbian bars and pride and dance parties and all that this city has to offer, these places where my Muslimness, my brownness feel acutely out of place. These places where, once, a white lesbian once petted my hijab like I was an exotic creature, where this other time, a Moroccan bouncer looked me up and down and said, "What are you doing here, sister?"

It has taken a while to find this group of queer Muslims who have become family.

I share, too. It's my first time reading my writing aloud. I'm nervous and more than once I bumble the words, but the audience had been supportive, and it energizes me as I bike up the Manhattan bridge. Peddle and puff on this rusty, heavy bike that has lived better days.

I decided to read a safe piece. Short and straightforward, about brown aunties and my faltering Urdu. Gets a few laughs, easy.

But all I can think of as I make my way up my favorite bridge, my thighs burning, is what I had wanted to share. It's been a rough week, and I'm reeling still. A few days ago, a man — seemingly ordinary, in a Yankees T-shirt — stood in the middle of the bike lane as I approached. I figured he'd move out of the way, and he did, but not before I'd almost reached him, not before he'd stuck out his arm and pretended to punch me. Terrorist, he hissed after me. I wobbled, but caught myself. I pedaled away as fast as I could. And started wearing a helmet when I bike. Then, yesterday, the mailroom guy at work who I make small talk with stopped me and asked what I think about ISIS. *Muslims think they're evil too, right: You think they're evil too, right?* I broke my rule of refusing to apologize for things I am not part of because he was holding my packages hostage.

I pause at the top of the bridge to catch my breath. There's a viewing deck there, a small semi-circle to rest tired legs, and I get off and sit on the ground with the city splayed before me. The East River underneath, a black abyss, and above it, the city. The buildings lining the curve of the island, the lights in windows in the buildings and the people wrapping up their Saturday nights and the people still working and the people cleaning the hallways and the bathrooms for the next day and the people driving cabs to take tipsy revelers home — the beauty of this manmade ecosystem that somehow works, the beauty of this frenzy.

This beauty, accessible to me so tenuously, depending on which of my identities is showing. I'm getting ready to graduate, trying to figure out what's next and it hits me again how soon I might have to leave this city, this country. So I do that thing I've been doing to cope, which is to pretend: that my visa doesn't expire soon, that I don't have a set number of days I can be unemployed before I must leave, that I might not be able to build on these roots I've started to send into the ground. I pretend that none of this exists and get back on my bike. Speed through the last level stretch of this bridge, and take my feet off the pedals into free fall.

VI.

Look at this city. Look at this city from here. Look at the way it rises and wanes, peeps in between trees, houses, highways.

I'm on a bus, on my way back from visiting my nearest of kin this side of the ocean — distant relatives that I only half know. It's been a weekend of straight-backed chairs and playing straight. The tedium of a conservative suburb so white that it sharpens the contours of my brownness, so small that it is impossible to go to the grocery store without running into someone my relatives know.

Approach from the north, through the Bronx. Brief glimpses between fences of houses with lawns and driveways with cars, the city a comfortable commutable whisper. Merge on to 278 West, and the neighborhood is laid bare. Tall, crumbling apartment buildings framed by exposed power lines and smoke stacks. Factories missing windows, faded graffiti, all remnants of the black and brown communities torn up and replaced with highways for easy access into the city.

I'm ready to be back. Lighter with each mile covered, my constant, controlled panic lifting as we travel closer. Easing the yearning of my heart for this city.

On to the Triborough bridge. The city laid out in front, the luxurious waterfront apartments of the Upper East Side, the wealth of the island rising, rising into the pinks, the blues, the striking purples of the sunset sky. (And just behind, the jail complex of Rikers Island. A pen for the poorest, the most marginalized who cannot afford bail. Waiting for trials, waiting for acquittals, those who live, die, give birth while waiting in this monstrosity.)

I'm ready to be back in this city, in this fragile balance I know. In this city where anonymity is not a luxury, where queerness thrives, but brownness is marginalized, criminalized, surveilled.

Circle this city. And look at this city from here. Through Queens, with its buildings close enough to touch. Parks and playground and brown families wheeling double strollers home. Peek inside apartments in Brooklyn. The windows framing lives playing in parallel. Circle this city and tighten the gyre. Turn onto the Brooklyn Bridge. A last view up the river — the sky settles into a deep cobalt blue and the lights in the windows in the buildings flicker on.

In the beginning, there was a plane; and then there was an airport. And then there was a language. And then there was a city that taught me to live. This queer city, this brown city — this queer brown city. Finally, finally, I am home.

THE MILITARY COMMISSIONS AT GUANTANAMO

MOLLY McCLOSKEY

When I visited Guantanamo Bay in September, and in the weeks after when this essay was written, no one I knew believed that Donald Trump would be elected. The detention facilities seemed to be winding, inexorably, down. The military commissions themselves looked like an experiment that had not played out as planned and that, whatever their eventual outcomes, provided a template on how not to do things going forward. I was producing, I thought, a snapshot from the end of an era. Now, the future of both the detention facilities and the commissions is more uncertain than ever, and the essay may instead be a snapshot of a system that is about to enjoy a second act.

- March 10, 2017

1. Getting There

The departure-lounge vibe at Andrews Air Force Base felt like the beginning of a package holiday, one taken with a group of highly intelligent and mutually suspicious people.

On board the Miami Air charter flight, the judge got the front row, and all the other parties — prosecution, defense, media, NGO observers, and the victims and family members — clustered together in our assigned sections. When we landed at Guantanamo Bay Naval Base, I asked the young American sailor who checked my passport how was he doing, and he said: "I'm living the Gitmo dream."

Indeed, it did feel like a strange dream, our ferry ride across the bay, over water so blue and beautiful it was almost painful to behold, on the far side of which was one of the world's most notorious prisons. The heaven/hell dissonance of arrival there had never, I imagined, been lost on anyone.

I was in Guantanamo to attend three days of pre-trial hearings in the case of Abd al-Rahim al-Nashiri, the Saudi national accused of orchestrating the October 2000 suicide bombing of the USS Cole when it was docked at Aden, Yemen. Seventeen American sailors died in

ENTRANCE TO DETENTION FACILITIES CAMPS 5 AND 6, GUANTANAMO BAY / PHOTO COURTESY OF MOLLY McCLOSKEY

TENT CITY, CAMP JUSTICE, GUANTANAMO BAY / PHOTO COURTESY OF MOLLY McCLOSKEY

the attack, and 39 others on board were injured. If convicted, Nashiri will face the death penalty.

As of September 6, 2016, the day I arrived, Nashiri was one of 61 detainees left at Guantanamo, down from an estimated 677 in 2003 (a total of 780 men have been held there). Twenty-one of those remaining had been cleared for release, another five were waiting to hear if they'd be cleared. Twenty-five were so-called "forever prisoners," not charged with anything but deemed too dangerous to release. Only 10 were or had been before the military commissions, charged with war crimes.

The commissions were established by executive order in the aftermath of the 9/11 attacks for the purpose of trying "enemy combatants" — non-US citizens deemed to be members of al-Qaeda or otherwise presenting a terrorist threat to the United States — who the government accused of war crimes. But the commissions have been plagued by controversy since their inception, bogged down in dubious legal rationales and tainted by the torture of those facing charges.

On the tarmac at the airport, Nashiri's lead lawyer, Richard Kammen, had shown me his stuffed kangaroo, which he'd brought to court on occasion and placed on the defense table. As he pulled it out of his backpack, he said, "So that I never forget and the team never forgets what these proceedings really are."

2. Tent City

The landscape was baked dry. Everywhere had the feel of a deserted fairground. I slept in a tent, in the so-called Tent City, rows of canvas polytunnel-shaped units located in Camp Justice, the area of the naval base where the hearings take place.

Each tent contained six beds, separated by plywood boards and curtains, and had a large, noisy AC unit affixed to its exterior. The tents were kept ludicrously cold to deter the iguanas, banana rats, and mosquitoes. On hot Cuban nights, I wore flannel pajamas and socks to bed. Toilets and showers were in adjacent tents, and when I stumbled out at 3:00 a.m. to use the toilet, I experienced an inversion of the normal camping-style experience: instead of going from my warm bed into the cold night, I stepped from my refrigerated tent into the humid dark.

Most of the 100 tents were empty. I had just one tentmate — Carol Rosenberg, from the *Miami Herald*. When it became known, in 2002, that the first detainees were on their way to Guantanamo, Carol's boss at the *Herald* told her to come down and stay till it was over. She was there the day the first detainees arrived, and has been covering the story since.

Carol has written on every aspect of the place, including the base's traffic court, mordantly called by some Guantanamo's *functioning* court. She told me she'd seen as many as 57 press people staying in Tent City. But there had been many nights over the past several years when she was the only journalist here. Gitmo is a story many media outlets — and most Americans — have largely forgotten.

3. Torture

Abd al-Rahim al-Nashiri was captured by the CIA in Dubai in November 2002. Much of what we know about what happened to him over the next few years can be found in the heavily redacted, 525-page executive summary of the study conducted by Senate Select Committee on Intelligence (SSCI) of the CIA's Detention and Interrogation program, colloquially known as the Torture Report.

Nashiri was detained at various CIA black sites for four years, where he was subjected to beatings, sleep deprivation, and waterboarding. He was threatened with a handgun and a drill, regularly forced into "stress positions" (at one point prompting a medical officer to worry about his arms bring dislocated), told that his mother was going to be brought in (her rape was implied), and subjected to "forced bathing" with a wire brush.

For a time, Nashiri was kept at a black site codenamed COBALT in Afghanistan. COBALT suffered from a particular lack of oversight in a program not generally strong on oversight. It reportedly operated in total darkness, with the guards wearing headlamps. Detainees were kept naked and shackled to the wall or to a bar on the ceiling. One CIA interrogator stated that some of the detainees there "literally looked like a dog that had been kenneled." When their cell doors were opened, "they cowered."

During a hunger strike protest, Nashiri was subjected to "rectal rehydration." A nutrient supplement was infused into him "in a forward-facing position with head lower than torso." The CIA has defended rectal rehydration as a medical technique, though medical experts say that, as the rectum is not an efficient way to absorb nutrients, the procedure is never medically necessary. It can result in damage to the colon, food rotting inside the digestive tract, and an inflamed or prolapsed rectum.

(One of the 9/11 defendants, Mustafa al-Hawsawi — accused of helping the hijackers with money and other logistical support — suffered chronic bleeding, an anal fissure, and rectal prolapse. Hawsawi always had a cushion on his chair in the military commissions courtroom — the reasons for which were apparently not broached even with his lawyer, Walter Ruiz, until after the Torture Report came out. Ruiz called what happened to his client "sodomy," and said that after a bowel movement, Hawsawi had to manually "reinsert parts of his anus back into his anal cavity.")

In 2003, the CIA's chief of interrogations, whose presence had prompted Nashiri to "tremble in fear," became concerned about him. He did not believe that Nashiri was withholding significant information, and, having received a proposed interrogation plan for him, informed the front office of the Counterterrorism Center that he would "no longer be associated in any way with the interrogation program due to serious reservation[s] about the current state of affairs." In the same email, he said the program was "a train wreak [*sic*] waiting to happen and I intend to get the hell off the train before it happens." But instead of easing up on Nashiri, HQ approved the continuation of his torture.

Dr. Sondra Crosby, a professor of medicine at Boston University and a consultant to Physicians for Human Rights, was allowed to examine Nashiri at Guantanamo on more than one occasion. Crosby, who has served as an expert witness for the defense, concluded that Nashiri was suffering from complex PTSD "as a result of extreme physical, psychological, and sexual torture inflicted upon him by the United States," and was "most likely irreversibly

TOP: CAMP IGUANA, GUANTANAMO BAY, BOTTOM: CAMP IGUANA / PHOTOS COURTESY OF MOLLY McCLOSKEY

CAMP IGUANA / PHOTO COURTESY OF MOLLY McCLOSKEY

damaged." She added that in her many years of experience treating torture victims from around the world, Nashiri "presents as one of the most severely traumatized individuals" she had ever seen.

4. The Charges

Aside from the Cole bombing charges, Nashiri is also facing charges related to the attack in 2002 on the French MV Limburg off the coast of Yemen, in which one crew member died and 12 others were injured.

Two years ago, the judge presiding over Nashiri's case, Colonel Vance Spath, dismissed the Limburg charges for lack of jurisdiction. The chief prosecutor appealed, resulting in an 18-month recess, during which the special appeals court created by Congress for the military commissions reversed Spath's ruling and reinstated the charges. But Kammen, looking to a recent Supreme Court ruling dealing with extraterritorial crime, was going to argue that the Limburg charges should, once again, be dismissed.

You may wonder why so much energy is going into what seems a mere addendum to the case. If 17 American military deaths are not enough to convict Nashiri, why would one Bulgarian death on a French-flagged tanker matter?

It may end up mattering a lot. There has been a running debate about whether Nashiri is even in the right court.

The military commissions have jurisdiction only over war crimes, and while the US government contends that it was in armed conflict with al-Qaeda for some years before 9/11, citing Osama bin Laden's fatwa in 1996 and the 1998 Kenya and Tanzania embassy bombings, the United States's official "declaration of war" is dated September 14, 2001. If the Limburg charges are dropped, and it is ultimately decided that the United States was not at war with al-Qaeda when the USS Cole was bombed in October 2000, then Nashiri shouldn't be sitting before the military commissions at all but in federal court.

On August 30, 2016, the US Court of Appeals for the District of Columbia Circuit abstained from ruling on Nashiri's petition to halt his trial by military commission, leaving the trial to play out in Guantanamo. The case could yet end up back in the DC Circuit on appeal. Though there would be serious issues related to double jeopardy, it's conceivable that seven to 10 years from now, Nashiri could be facing another death-penalty trial in federal court for the Cole bombings.

If Nashiri is acquitted at Guantanamo, there is no reason to assume he will be released. According to the US government, he was a high-ranking member of al-Qaeda, and a leader of his own cell; he is alleged to have supported, logistically or financially, as many as a dozen plots to attack US and Western interests, including one to sink a US ship in the Strait of Hormuz; a plot to use an explosives-filled airplane against Western warships at Port Rashid, Dubai; and a plot to blow up the US Embassy in Sanaa. Nashiri's Department of Defense Detainee Assessment states that he was "so dedicated to jihad that he reportedly received injections to promote impotence" rather than being distracted by women.

On the basis of these accusations, the US government could continue to detain Nashiri, post-acquittal, as an enemy combatant, shifting him into the category of "forever prisoner," what Kammen calls "a euphemism for people who the CIA doesn't want to be talking about what happened to them."

5. Court

We assembled in the morning outside the courtroom. Security screening was similar to an airport but a good bit more amiable.

Journalists, visiting lawyers, and NGO observers watched the proceedings from a viewing gallery that was separated from the courtroom by soundproof glass. There was also a section in the gallery for victims and family members — the VFM, as they're called — which could be made private from the other observers by a curtain. That week, the VFM numbered eight: the mother of a sailor who died on the USS Cole was there with her cousin, and the father of another victim had come with his brother; there were also two men who'd been serving on the Cole the day it was attacked, accompanied by their wives.

Nashiri was already seated when we entered the gallery. He looked surprisingly animated: smiling, chatty, joking with the guards. When a female paralegal joined the defense table, he stood and embraced her. Dressed in loose-fitting white shirt and pants, he seemed physically at ease.

Those of us in the gallery could see, but not hear, the proceedings as they unfolded on the other side of the soundproof glass. We could also follow them on screens above our heads, an audio-visual transmission that was on a 40-second delay, to guard against a spill of classified information. It sounds like a disorienting set-up but it was simply like watching everything in ongoing instant replay.

I already knew that Kammen and the chief prosecutor, General Mark Martins, existed in parallel worlds. What I'd heard Kammen refer to as "a farce," Martins had called a "sharply adversarial process," and "a system to be given the greatest credit." Not all of the military prosecutors have shared Martin's view. Over the last several years, seven lawyers from the prosecution side have resigned or requested transfer because of concerns about the ethics or legality of the commissions.

A graduate of West Point and Harvard, Martins helped draft the Military Commissions Act of 2009, which improved protections for defendants — for instance, restricting the use of coerced and hearsay evidence, and providing greater defense counsel resources — but which still falls far short of granting the due process rights afforded defendants under the US Constitution. (In 2008, the Supreme Court ruled in Boumediene v. Bush that parts of the 2006 Military Commissions Act were unconstitutional because they restricted detainees' use of habeas corpus and access to federal courts. The ruling determined that detainees had the right to challenge their detention in federal court via habeas corpus. The Military Commissions Act of 2009 was, in part, a response to Boumediene v. Bush.) When Martins accepted the appointment of chief prosecutor in 2011, it was with the stated intention of demonstrating to the public that the commissions could be a vehicle for real justice.

In court, Martins tended toward the impassive, whereas Kammen's affect was that of a man perpetually flabbergasted. Judge Spath, for his part, had the air of an affably world-weary game show host. He was relatively informal, droll without seeming blasé or insincere. He gave the impression that the three parties — the prosecution, the defense, and himself — were there to get a job done, and while it was not a particularly pleasant job, if they put their heads together, they might see the damn thing through.

Pre-trial hearings at Guantanamo have involved a lot of motions filed by the defense arguing for either abatement or dismissal because of aspects of the commissions process they deem unfair or illegal. Some motions have been in response to flagrant acts of misconduct, such as the FBI's attempt in 2014 to turn a member of Ramzi bin al-Shibh's defense team into an informant; others have been closer to Hail Marys. But all have aimed at chipping away at a flawed system.

One of that morning's motions was a request for abatement until two attorneys appointed to the Nashiri team could get their security clearances. Everyone in the courtroom required fairly high-level clearance, and the two women had been waiting for about a year, during which time they'd been unable to sit in on certain conversations, view classified documents, or come to Guantanamo to meet their client. Nashiri, it seemed, had questioned their very existence.

6. "...torture, or whatever we're going to call it."

In a Q&A published in *The New Yorker* a few years ago, Amy Davidson discussed torture with Jose Rodriguez, who was director of the CIA's Counterterrorism Center during the rendition, detention, and interrogation (RDI) period.

Rodriguez said to her, "I really resent you using the word 'torture' time and time again [...] look, this is not torture." He preferred "enhanced interrogation." Rodriguez's main argument seemed to be that (a) torture is illegal, (b) what the CIA did was legal because the Department of Justice declared it so, and (c) therefore what the CIA did couldn't be torture. To which Davidson replied: "Does that come across as defining away torture?"

As sugar-coating euphemisms go, the use of "enhanced" seems particularly egregious; I can think of no instance in day-to-day discourse in which *enhanced* doesn't have positive connotations. Who doesn't want their experience to be enhanced?

I got the sense that even Judge Spath was a little weary of the semantics: "enhanced interrogation or torture, or whatever we're going to call it," he said in court.

Most of the time we didn't call it anything, this thing that hummed through Camp Justice, as constitutive of the atmosphere as the humidity itself and, to a large extent, why all of this was here. Had things unfolded otherwise in the aftermath of 9/11, these men could have ended up in federal court, or even in a military commission on the US mainland. But when rapport-building gave way to torture, and a lot of tainted evidence was amassed, the Bush administration needed a place to put people they'd tortured and, in some cases, were still torturing, and — eventually, perhaps — to try them.

One of the issues to be litigated in these cases is the question of just what it means to say that statements are free of the taint of torture. This was touched on during the Nashiri hearings in relation to Ahmed Haza al-Darbi, who is expected to testify against Nashiri.

Darbi negotiated a plea deal related to charges stemming from the attack on the Limburg, though his sentencing won't take place until at least 2017, after any testimony. Part of the plea deal was his agreement not to sue the United States over the conditions of his confinement.

Darbi arrived at Guantanamo in 2002, having been tortured at Bagram Air Force Base in Afghanistan. Darbi made statements in 2002. He also made "clean" statements in 2007. And he will make more statements in the actual courtroom, should he testify there. On day three of the Nashiri hearings, a defense attorney, Lieutenant Commander Jennifer Pollio, argued that "treatment received in 2002" was, and will be, relevant to statements from all three of these periods. "The impact of torture is long-lasting … these things don't happen in a void."

Indeed, they don't. How long might the effects of torture be said to linger? How does that length of time relate to the nature and the extent of the abuse, and to individual factors that affect subsequent adjustment? Isn't it possible that statements — partially or entirely inaccurate ones — that I've made under duress are statements that later, although I'm no longer in danger or obvious distress, I've come myself to believe? How can these questions and their answers be quantified in a meaningful and accurate way?

The day of my arrival on the base, we went to the supermarket to stock up on food for the week. The supermarket is in the Navy Exchange complex, or the NEX; nearby is a Subway, a McDonald's, a video store, and various other strip-mall amenities. Carol, who must've shown journalists around the NEX supermarket a thousand times, showed me around the NEX supermarket. In the yoghurt aisle, a gray-haired man, who looked for all the world like someone just in from a relaxing round of golf, smiled benignly at us. When he'd wheeled his cart away, Carol said, "That's the judge. It's like small-town America here."

In the supermarket, I had that feeling — unsupportable here — that one has when happening on a source of plenty in a place of scarcity, and I had to refrain from scrambling around excitedly and buying way too much.

On the way out, through the wi-fi-equipped patio, which was full of people clustered at tables and glued to their phones, and looked remarkably like the real world, I said to Carol: "Wasn't it strange, in the early days, to come grocery shopping and know that a few miles down the road people were being tortured?"

Indeed it was, she said, and more horrific still when the three detainees were found dead in their cells in 2006. (The official government line was that the three men had killed themselves by hanging in a suicide pact, but some journalists and lawyers investigating since have argued that there are a number of inconsistencies in the government's account.)

It was hard to feel that horror, though. The cognitive dissonance that arose from the nearness of a suburban-Florida-style shopping mall to a former black site dissipated quickly, and what lingered was a grim, low-frequency bad vibe, made grimmer by the fact that it was frankly easy to get on with the day while breathing that air. There I was, squeezing oranges for ripeness while down the road a man was having to manually reinsert part of his anus. Two realities normally worlds apart — my comfortable existence and the heinous deeds done in the name of protecting that existence — were suddenly in close proximity. Some of those heinous deeds may well have bolstered my security; others seriously undermined it.

TOP: CAMP IGUANA, BOTTOM: CAMP IGUANA / PHOTOS COURTESY OF MOLLY McCLOSKEY

What do I know? What do I want to know?

When asked about the methods used to "protect the nation," Rodriguez had said, "I don't subscribe to the notion that the American people need to know everything." He might as easily have said *want* to know everything.

I was given — *even at Guantanamo* — the luxury of looking the other way. Some of that luxury was mandatory. In the case of Camp 7, where the "high-value" detainees are held, its location and whatever goes on there were hidden from me: classified.

By the end of day two, having dinner in O'Kelly's Irish Pub, eating fish tacos, surrounded by big-screen TVs broadcasting sports and news, a large crowd of Filipino migrant workers playing bingo in the huge room adjacent to the pub, I'd already given up asking Carol about the weirdness of grocery shopping and torture juxtaposed. Whatever there was to say about the air of this place seemed either banal or inexpressible.

When the detention center, or the detainees themselves, were spoken about by anyone in an official government capacity, it was in the form, not surprisingly, of talking points — mantras of the "humane and legitimate" detention that rules the day, canned responses that more often than not ended up in the cul-de-sac of: "I don't know. That's a policy decision."

Carol could be counted on to throw a wrench into this polite discourse, remarking bluntly, just by the way, on how so-and-so got such-and-such shoved into an orifice. (In the more bureaucratic language of the SSCI report: "[l]ater that same day, Majid Kahn's 'lunch tray' of hummus, pasta with sauce, nuts, and raisins was 'pureed' and rectally infused." *Later that same day*?) Carol's comment — delivered as I was enjoying the view out the window of our climate-controlled van, the bay shimmering fantastically in the sun, our driver a National Guardsman who seemed so laid back and conflict-averse I actually asked him how on earth he survived in a war zone (he said the "California" manner was a good thing in a place like Iraq, because such people worked better on a team) — *pinged* in my consciousness like the snapped fingers of a hypnotist, jarring me from my talking-point-induced stupor.

Oh *yes*, I thought. Oh yes. *There* is *that*.

7. "...actually, I think that's my divorce trial..."

If anything offered a glimpse into why the commissions at Guantanamo — this messy hybrid system that is short on precedent and full of fuzzy rules — are so gummed up, it was the testimony of Lieutenant Commander Stephen Gill. For a few months in 2015, Gill had worked for the Office of the Convening Authority, which functions in military justice a little like a tribal elder: when a crime is committed within the ranks, the convening authority convenes a court — a military commission — to try the case. At Guantanamo, the authority is responsible for the overall management of the commissions process, including logistics, referring charges to trial, negotiating pre-trial agreements, and choosing the jury pool of military officers. There is no parallel body in the federal courts system, and the defense has argued that the convening authority's dual administrative and prosecutorial role violates due process.

In early 2015, the convening authority was embroiled in controversy when the Department of Defense, based on the authority's recommendations, issued an order requiring all commissions judges to move to Guantanamo and to live there until their cases were concluded. Given the unattractiveness of that prospect, the order would have provided clear incentive for judges to either wrap things up quickly or resign from their cases. The defense cried foul, as did the judges, who ruled it an attempt at unlawful influence. The Department of Defense quickly revoked the order. The senior Pentagon official who headed the authority resigned in the fallout.

Judge Spath issued an order disqualifying the convening authority lawyers involved from having anything more to do with the Nashiri case. Gill, who was unconnected with the controversy, had been called by the defense to testify that the lawyers Spath had disqualified had continued to involve themselves in the Nashiri case.

Via a video feed from Alexandria, Virginia, Gill explained that he had observed a pattern of conduct in violation of the order, and had begun to complain. When he was stonewalled, he went all the way up the chain of command to the chief prosecutor, Mark Martins, the then chief defense counsel, and a relevant person at the Department of Defense.

In late April, Gill was fired from the convening authority. The narrative that emerged from the defense's questioning was one of clear cause and effect: Gill was a whistleblower who'd been fired because of his complaints. Gill was a foot soldier in the fight for integrity. If he seemed a bit peevish and defensive, it was with good and righteous reason.

But during cross-examination, a prosecutor, Lieutenant Paul Morris, asked Gill if he wasn't in fact fired because of concerns among his superiors over his security clearance being renewed? And hadn't he tried to get his wife to drop a "restraining order" she had against him because he too was concerned about his clearance?

Morris then transmitted an email for Gill to read, sent by Gill to his wife, who had presumably given it to the prosecution. (Gill, we learned, had been involved in a rather ugly divorce for the last three years.) In the email, Gill said that his wife should tell their daughters that their college education would have been paid for but for their mother's refusal to drop the restraining order, thus preventing their father from getting the security clearance he needed to continue the job to earn the money to pay the college tuition.

This wasn't good, and Gill, who was growing sweatier, made things arguably worse by saying he didn't actually believe what he wrote but was only trying to "strong-arm" his wife into "retracting her false allegations" — using "a hardball litigation tactic against an opposing party."

There was squirming in the gallery.

The prosecution moved on — to Gill's reckless driving violations, to what he had or hadn't reported on his security clearance questionnaire, to whether in his hometown newspaper he'd overstated his role in prosecuting terrorists in Afghanistan. And what about all those civil suits he'd filed? Against the Navy Federal Credit Union and the Commonwealth of Massachusetts; against the Navy itself, for $1 million for emotional distress after he'd been let go from a civilian contract in 2004. Had he sued Chrysler for breach of warranty?

"I sure did," he said. "I bought a car that was in the repair shop 38 times in six months..."

OUTSIDE THE JERK SHACK RESTAURANT / PHOTO COURTESY OF MOLLY McCLOSKEY

The VFM were, somehow, braving it out. I imagined this excursion into the less salubrious aspects of Gill's life — illuminating though the larger point may ultimately be about the malfunctions of the military commissions and the convening authority's attempted meddling — was excruciating for them, a reminder of the fact that we were nowhere near a trial, let alone a conviction.

Just before the judge excused us, he suggested a date for a session some weeks hence to continue with Gill's testimony, to which Gill responded: "actually, I think that's my divorce trial..."

8. What's Wrong With Federal Court?

Given that 17 years after the Cole bombing and 16 years after 9/11, we are still in the pre-trial phase, could federal court possibly be any less effective? The federal courts have a strong record with terrorism-related cases: prosecutors have won more than 350 convictions since 2001. The military commissions, by comparison, have completed just eight cases; three of the convictions have been overturned in their entirety and one has been partially overturned.

Federal court prosecutions include that of the only person yet tried in relation to 9/11 — Zacarias Moussaoui, who was arrested before the attacks after he aroused suspicion at a flight school in Minneapolis when he paid in cash and only wanted to learn how to take off and land. Moussaoui is now serving six life sentences. Other convicted terrorists include Richard Reid (the Shoe Bomber), Umar Farouk Abdulmutallab (the Underwear Bomber), four men behind the World Trade Center truck bombing in 1993, several men involved in the embassy bombings in Kenya and Tanzania, and Boston Marathon bomber Dzhokhar Tsarnaev, who passed only two years between arrest and conviction. All of these men are at so-called supermax prisons in the United States, where they cost the taxpayer about $75,000 per year, far less than the estimated $11 million a year it costs to detain one person at Guantanamo.

But since 2010, Congress has banned the use of any federal funds to transfer detainees to the United States or to hold them here. Many lawyers claim that the avoidance of federal court is almost all to do with the CIA wanting to keep details of the torture program under wraps. But given that a lot of material related to torture has already become available, albeit in heavily redacted form, one wonders if the government wouldn't be better off just lancing the boil and getting all this over with. But various issues make this an unattractive option.

One is that additional details that could then come out about the torture program may not simply be more of the same. Kammen has called the executive summary a "very sanitized version of the truth," while a December op-ed in *The New York Times* written by two former senators said that the full report contains "volumes of new information."[1]

There is also the possibility that individuals contracted by the CIA, as well as agency

1 "The Torture Report Must Be Saved," December 9, 2016, by Carl Levin and Jay Rockefeller. Levin was chairman of the Senate Armed Services Committee, and Rockefeller chairman of the SSCI.

employees, could be called upon in federal court to testify — which is exactly what happened recently in a Guantanamo-related case. In 2015, the American Civil Liberties Union filed a lawsuit on behalf of three former detainees against James Mitchell and Bruce Jessen, the ex-US military psychologists contracted by the CIA to design and run the RDI program. Jessen and Mitchell are being sued for torture, non-consensual human experimentation, and war crimes. The trial is schedule for June 2017. On October 4, 2016, a federal judge ruled that Jose Rodriguez and John Rizzo, the CIA's former acting general counsel, will be compelled to answer questions under oath about the RDI program. It is unprecedented in the country's history for a top-ranking CIA official to be deposed on operational information by a private party, and it just the sort of airing the CIA doesn't want.

9. The Windshield Tour

I took a "windshield tour" of the detention complex. I expected it to be a drive-by, chop-chop sort of outing, in which we'd be discouraged from looking too closely at anything as we whizzed past, but the tour was far more leisurely than I'd imagined. It felt oddly like one of those aimless road trips from my youth, or like an indie short, but with lots of concertina wire.

We parked first outside the entrance to Camps 5 and 6. Philip Crowther, a radio and TV journalist, set up his camera gear. We were both immediately struck by the red US mailbox, a flash of color in an otherwise baked-dull landscape. It had the word "Amnesty" on it. I wondered for a moment if it was a cruel joke — as though the detainees might mail their letters to Amnesty International right there — but it turned out to be a drop box for things like lighters and cigarettes that aren't allowed inside the camp.

Camp 5 was then being repurposed into a medical clinic for low-value detainees at a cost of $8.4 million; construction was expected to be completed in about a year. It seemed a lot of money to sink into a place whose population was shrinking, but the budgetary decision went back a couple of years. Our public affairs guide, Captain John Filostrat of the Joint Task Force (JTF), which oversees the detention facilities, said that the JTF's "ultimate goal is to close the detention facility." When I asked him how that might change under a new administration, and he said that their position depended on "what the Commander-in-Chief wants," I suspect neither of us was seriously imagining a Trump victory.

Because of a federal preservation order that bans the destruction of evidence, documents, and information related to all sites where those who have been detained at Guantanamo have been held, the medical clinic was, according to Captain Filostrat, being constructed "around" the actual cells.[2]

There was little to see from outside but the guard tower and the rather grim-looking entrance — a lot of cyclone fencing covered by green canvas. Guards were visible behind the fencing, but we had to be careful their faces didn't appear in any pictures we took. (Later,

2 This issue has been a source of controversy. A recent government filing to the District Court in DC advised the Court that the FBI would be creating "digital recordings" that could then be turned into 3-D mock-ups of certain areas of Camp 5 in order to maintain a record of those facilities. And, in early 2016, defense teams learned that Judge Pohl, in response to top-secret prosecution filings, had allowed the prosecution to destroy evidence related to a former CIA black site.

when our photos and film were vetted, I had to crop my long-distance shots because they showed a lock in a door.)

As we snapped photos from across the road, a military vehicle paused politely to allow us to finish, and it was almost impossible not to imagine that this place might one day be a tourist destination, an option on a package holiday to Cuba. More notorious prisons have met a similar end, and already there was a strange sense of slippage in the air. Gitmo T-shirts and mugs were available at the base stores, including a JTF GTMO DETAINEE OPERATIONS T-shirt depicting a silhouetted guard shack and a roll of barbed wire.

Gitmo-as-detention-center and Gitmo-as-entertainment were blurring. When I Googled images of Camp X-Ray — the cluster of cages and shacks where the first detainees were held — what I got by default were not pictures of the detention center complex but rather dozens of images from the film *Camp X-Ray*, in which Kristen Stewart plays a US soldier who forms a friendship with a detainee. What I also saw in my searches were lots of smiling group photos, many in front of the Camp Justice sign and, in the case of the Atlanta Falcons cheerleaders, taken while touring Camps 5 and 6. A recent John Oliver sketch on why the US government should close Gitmo contained a clip of what Oliver described as news crews touring a Camp 5 cell "like it's a million-dollar listing." A young military man, his face hidden, explained that a typical cell in Camp 5 had 95 square feet of living space, met all American Correctional Association standards, and had access to amenities such as the prison library.

Our little group piled back into the van, and we moved on to Camp Iguana, which for years was home to 22 ethnic Uighur Muslims from China. Most were captured in Afghanistan in 2001, turned in to the US military for the now famous $5,000 bounty. They said they'd gone to Afghanistan to escape persecution in China. Even after the United States determined that they had no links to al-Qaeda and were not a threat, they couldn't be sent back to China because they were likely to be tortured there. Over the years, they'd been scattered between five countries, until finally, in 2013, the last three were transferred to Slovakia.

The Camp Iguana compound sat on the very edge of a cliff overlooking the sea, a cluster of low-slung buildings, inching toward dilapidation, behind cyclone fencing. The JTF logo with the bald eagle was peeling off the signboard. The heaven/hell of the Gitmo gestalt was there cast in stark relief — all that barbed wire and the stunning Caribbean just below. Philip remarked that at least these detainees had a view, but the captain corrected him: there was heavy netting in place when the camp was occupied.

Camp Iguana radiated a dark energy. It wasn't just abandoned; there was something tainted about its bleakness. The sign on the locked gate that said simply "Off Limits" called to mind contaminated land, as though a chemical spill had occurred there. Camp Iguana might be how all of this will feel in decades to come, if it isn't crowded by tourists paying top dollar for a night in an authentic disused cell.

10. The Social Contract

Chief Prosecutor Martins was given to emphasizing that the charges against Nashiri were "only allegations," that the accused was "presumed innocent unless and until proven guilty." The victims and family members said otherwise, and they spoke, at least those who were there that week, with one voice. They were certain that Nashiri was guilty, and they blamed the defense and their "delaying tactics" — what a 9/11 family member called "judicial jihad" — for the way the case has dragged on. But they were adamant that they were going to see it through.

"I'm here so al-Nashiri sees my ass every time," said Joe Pelly, who was on the Cole the day it was hit. The emotion among them was still incredibly raw. At the press conference, a number of them were in tears.

Let us assume for a moment that Nashiri is guilty, and that he was responsible for the deaths of 17 sailors who were not engaged in active combat at the time of the attack. What is the problem — as one of the family members asked, rhetorically, at an informal roundtable — with torturing him? Wasn't the killing of those sailors and the pain inflicted on their loved ones a form of torture? Wasn't the PTSD that Pelly lived with "every friggin' day" a form of torture? ("What I saw on board doesn't go away.") Saundra Flanagan, who lost her son in the attack and wore a T-shirt with his name on it, said wearily, "I've been hearing for 16 years about Mr. Nashiri's mental states." Back in the 1990s, President Bill Clinton looked her in the eye and promised justice. Sometimes, in nightmares, she saw her son.

Cue John McCain, that strange star in our firmament, who can occasionally be counted on to depart from the Republican orthodoxy and go to bat for what he believes. McCain, who was tortured as a POW in Vietnam and so speaks with a moral authority on the subject that no other member of Congress can claim, has been vocal and consistent in his opposition to the CIA's torture program, and torture generally, as both morally debasing and ineffective. His oft-quoted lines float rightly free of any particular "they": "It's not about who they are. It's about who we are."

During our media roundtable with the family members and victims, James Parlier, who was on board the Cole and treated wounded sailors, said of Guantanamo: "It's unfortunate that some of those people did wind up here that probably weren't guilty and had to serve a lot of time, but this is war. It's like the people that get killed when a round goes off and you don't intend it."

Parlier described stories he'd heard of guards at Gitmo who had behaved with discipline and dignity in the face of provocations from detainees. "I was proud of them," he said, "for being able to grit their teeth and take it and do the right thing." He said that what we have learned through all of this "is that as American people we *are* humane."

The world may balk at the notion of Guantanamo as evidence of America's humanity, but I think what Parlier was gesturing toward was the rule of law: that abstraction that can protect us from our worst selves, and that has at its core the belief that there is something that takes precedence over an individual life.

The interdependence of the two — the concept and the singular, suffering individual — is paradoxical, for if there is something larger at stake than my own suffering or my life, and that something is the law, it is also true that the law is intimately connected to each individual life, and in fact would be meaningless without that referent; singular cases, after all, are what law is comprised of.

I may not call to mind what Parlier does to evidence some redemptive potential here. I

CABLE BEACH, GUANTANAMO BAY / PHOTO COURTESY OF MOLLY McCLOSKEY

may think instead of the recent federal court ruling in the ACLU case taken against the architects of the RDI program, the case that may yet give torture victims their day in court, hold some perpetrators accountable, and attest to the strengths of our federal judicial system. But I think we are looking in the same direction. I think we are acknowledging that, paradoxically, it is by submitting to an abstraction that we remain, or become again, humane.

11. Dear Amy

On October 7, I read four letters published in *The Washington Post*. They were written by Zayn al-Abidin Muhammad Husayn — better known as Abu Zubaydah — the so-called guinea pig, or "person zero," for the torture program.

Like Nashiri, Zubaydah is classed as a high-value detainee and kept in Camp 7; unlike Nashiri, Zubaydah has never been charged with anything and never appeared in court. In fact, until his Periodic Review Board[3] hearing in August, when reporters and human rights advocates watched a live video of the short unclassified part of the session, Zubaydah had not been seen in public since his capture in Pakistan in 2002. At that time, the Bush administration had regarded him as the first big catch in the post-9/11 manhunt and labeled him the number three man in al-Qaeda.

According to the SSCI report, the CIA detained Zubaydah for four years at black sites in Thailand, Poland, and elsewhere. He was first questioned by FBI agents using traditional rapport-building techniques. Ali Soufan, an Arabic-speaking FBI agent who had long worked on al-Qaeda, has always insisted that Zubaydah was cooperating with the FBI, providing valuable information, including identifying Khalid Sheikh Mohammed as the mastermind of the 9/11 attacks.

Over the protests of FBI agents, as well as some in the CIA, the agency — advised by Jessen and Mitchell — lobbied Washington for permission to move on to harsher methods. The interrogation team cabled an additional request: "in light of the planned psychological pressure techniques to be implemented, we need to get reasonable assurances that [Abu Zubaydah] will remain in isolation and incommunicado for the remainder of his life." Explicit assurances were provided a few days later.

Zubaydah was waterboarded 83 times, kept in a cramped box, subjected to sleep deprivation, shackled in stress positions, and slammed into a wall. He was subjected to approved and improvised forms of torture. In 2005, the CIA destroyed dozens of videotapes of his interrogations.

By that time, it had become clear that Zubaydah had never been a high-ranking member of al-Qaeda, but was rather — according to people like Ron Suskind, the Pulitzer Prize–winning journalist who has written extensively on US counterterrorism — more like a minor logistics man, a clerk. The US government has long since abandoned its initial

3 The Periodic Review Board is a panel composed of members of six security agencies that decides between continued detention or transfer to another country. On October 27, the Board announced that Zubaydah would remain detained in order to "protect against a continuing significant threat to the security of the United States."

assessment of Zubaydah.

In addition to six volumes of diaries written between 1990 and 2002, confiscated by the Americans when Zubaydah was captured, Zubaydah's lawyers say that their client wrote three more volumes in which he describes his torture in detail. These later accounts remain classified; his lawyers have seen only redacted copies of them. Zubaydah's mental and physical health has long been a matter of discussion. He sustained a head injury while fighting against the Russians in Afghanistan in the 1980s, and somewhere between his capture in 2002 and his arrival at Guantanamo he suffered the loss of an eye — possibly an existing infection that went untreated.

Because much of what is known or said about Zubaydah's health is still presumptively classified, one of his lawyers, Amy Jacobsen, wouldn't comment directly on it when we spoke over Skype in October, only to say that her client had suffered "hundreds of seizures" since he was brought to Guantanamo, and that "it is reasonable to expect, based on the torture he endured, that there's a connection" between the torture and the seizures.

Zubaydah was not allowed to speak during the public session of his hearing in August. Instead, a half-page statement about him, written by his government representatives, was read out on his behalf. The letters published in the *Post* therefore represent the first time Zubaydah's lawyers have been able to share a communication of his with the outside world. Here is one of the letters:

> Dear Amy:
>
> Here is what I think about the human mind:
>
> It is like a scale for weighing, which can measure up to 1 kilo only. It can be extremely precise, telling in fine detail to the hundredth and thousandth decimal place the weight of a beautiful diamond. But try to consider something too great, 10 kilos, 20 kilos, beyond its comprehension, and you will break the scale.
>
> So, too, for me: there are ideas which are beyond human comprehension and if we try to consider them with our 1 kilo scale, it will break the scale, by which I mean, it can make you crazy, or it will read at most a measure of 1 kilo, which is to say, give an inaccurate reading. Of course, this does not mean that we should stop searching and trying to comprehend, but as we do so, it must be understood within the limits of our scale.
>
> Zayn Husayn

BECKY KOLSRUD, 2014, *VEILED*, OIL ON CANVAS, 30 X 24 INCHES / COURTESY OF THE ARTIST AND JTT NEW YORK

CIVILITY

MAI DER VANG

What is it to swallow the glass
          and open within: a window.

   To vitamin our lives,
mirrors of each other

molded from   the shattered fingernails
of a saint.

            Are we a punctured
future built on roofless soil?

                They said to us: guard
the last water of its kind,

encrypt the history of its tribe
   as blink-beats.

      Then prepare for the assemblage
of disfiguration,

                and know why a maple's bark
can fit again together.

We must antler through
          not led by ones who curate blood.

     Take this our offering of audio
glands from the wings of a tree

thrusting a lament in the vortex
                           of a curing tune.

          We'll walk without steps to marry
the seams of the saola's wound,

  breathe as crescendos becoming
the armed   of a choiceless choir.

AND YET STILL MORE

MAI DER VANG

That refugees somewhere and everywhere are waiting
That the waiting suffocates the ankles
That the body cannot be fed from the waiting
That the spew of shrapnel from hubris tongues enact the waiting
That waiting is never certain of itself
That waiting could change its mind over-morning
That waiting won't change its mind
That elbows cradle the waiting at night
That all are conceived and born into waiting
That the waiting can span the range of two continents
That waiting is a kind of forgetting and forgetting is the sea
That waiting is a silent syllable in never mind
That even the dead wait
That waiting is not the same as faith
That not all waiting is created equal
That waiting drips from the sap-hammer of a noose
That waiting turns-to-hunger-turns-to-water-turns-to-going-turns-to-too-late
That a refugee somewhere is waiting
That a refugee everywhere is waiting
That waiting has no documentation of its own history
That so much waiting is enough to kill
That waiting took more than nine months to birth infinity
That refugees carry a surplus of waiting in plastic bags
That the ancestors wait
That waiting is given to refugees as a disease is given to the blood
That refugees wait
That all waiting floats into the exosphere
That refugee fathers sit outside of high schools waiting for the bell
That landmines excel at waiting

That a sleeping refugee is still waiting even in a state of dreaming
That most waiting happens in daylight
That wait and home are not spelled the same way
That the refugee industry is built on the business of waiting
That refugees are put somewhere to wait
That refugees are put everywhere to wait
That wait is the refugee
That a refugee is waiting
That waiting must go on
That there is yet more waiting
That add this portion of a little longer to the wait
That wait is the refugee
That wait still and still more
That yet even
That next year
That ever always
That the year after
That more
That now
Waiting

CONTRIBUTORS

Akhil Reed Amar is an American legal scholar, an expert on constitutional law and criminal procedure. Having been the Southmayd Professor of Law at Yale Law School, he was named the Sterling Professor of Law there in 2008. A *Legal Affairs* poll placed Amar among the top 20 contemporary US legal thinkers.

William Archila is a poet and teacher. He earned his MFA in poetry from the University of Oregon, where he was given the Fighting Fund Fellow Award. His first collection of poetry, *The Art of Exile* won an International Latino Book Award in 2010, an Emerging Writer Fellowship Award from the Writer's Center in Bethesda, MD, and was selected for The Fifth Annual Debut Poets Round Up" in Poets & Writers. His Second book, *The Gravedigger's Archaeology*, won the 2013 Letras Latinas/Red Hen Poetry Prize. He has been published in *American Poetry Review*, *The Georgia Review, Notre Dame Review, Copper Nickle as well as many others.*

Laura W. Brill is a media law and appellate litigator and a former law clerk to Justice Ruth Bader Ginsburg.

Erwin Chemerinsky is Dean and Distinguished Professor, Raymond Pryke Professor of First Amendment Law, University of California, Irvine School of Law. Author of 10 books, most recently: *Closing the Courthouse Door: How Your Constitutional Rights Became Unenforceable* (Yale UniversityPress 2017).

Don Franzen is a lawyer in Beverly Hills specializing in entertainment and business law. He has lectured on entertainment law at the Eastman School of Music, Santa Monica College's Academy of Entertainment and Technology, the Berklee School of Music in Valencia, Spain, and lectures at UCLA's Herb Albert School of Music, where he teaches two courses on the law and the music industry. He has published articles on legal issues in newspapers, magazines, and law journals. He serves on the board of the Los Angeles Opera and counts among his clients leading performers in opera, orchestral music, film, and the recording industries. He is the legal affairs editor for *Los Angeles Review of Books*.

Gil Garcetti was a prosecutor with the Los Angeles County District Attorney's office for 32 years, eight of which he was the elected District Attorney (1992-2000), Gil Garcetti oversaw 1100 prosecutors, placed a special focus on combatting domestic violence, and initiated specific programs designed to prevent crime. He also oversaw high profile prosecutions, such as the Menendez brothers, O.J. Simpson cases, and LAPD's Ramparts Division police abuse cases. After leaving office, he taught at Harvard University's Kennedy School of Government. He has also been a frequent speaker on his various photo projects, career change, the death penalty, and especially on empowering women and girls in West Africa. He has published seven books of photo essays and has had numerous exhibitions of his photography.

Juan Felipe Herrera is a former United States Poet Laureate. He has won awards from Guggenheim, PEN USA, PEN American Center, the Smithsonian, and the National Book Critics Circle, among others. He lives with his partner, poet and performance artist Margarita Robles, in Fresno, California, and is Professor Emeritus at the University of California, Riverside. He grew up in a migrant farmworker family and is the author of some 30 books of poetry, fiction, YA fiction, children's books, and nonfiction.

Lamya H is a queer Muslim writer living in New York City. Her work has appeared in *Salon, Vox, Black Girl Dangerous, Autostraddle*, and others. She was a Lambda Literary Fellow in 2015.

Fady Joudah has three collections of poetry and several volume of translations form the Arabic. *Textu*, is his latest from Copper Canyon Press. He was the recipient of the Yale Series in 2007 and a Guggenheim Fellowship in 2014.

Priyanka Kumar is author of the novel "Take Wing and Fly Here" and the writer/director of the documentary "The Song of the Little Road." She is a recipient of an Alfred P. Sloan Foundation Award, New Mexico/New Visions Governor's Award, Canada Council for the Arts Grant, Ontario Arts Council Literary Award, and an Academy of Motion Pictures Arts and Sciences Fellowship. She contributes to several publications including *The Washington Post* and *High Country News*.

Molly McCloskey is a fiction writer, memoirist, and essayist. Her novel, *Straying*, will be published by Scribner in 2018, and in the UK in 2017 under the title *When Light is Like Water*. She lives in Washington, DC.

Ameena Mirza Qazi is the Executive Director of the Los Angeles chapter of the National Lawyers Guild. A civil rights attorney and activist, Ameena has worked on free speech, social and economic justice, discrimination, First Amendment, equal protection, and procedural due process issues. She is the former Deputy Executive Director and Staff Attorney for the Council on American-Islamic Relations—Greater Los Angeles Area Chapter (CAIR-LA), the largest American Muslim civil rights and advocacy group. Ameena has clerked with the United Auto Workers legal department, as well as the Wayne State University Disability Rights Clinic and the Civil Rights Litigation. She is also proud to be on the advisory board of the South Asian Network (SAN) and the boards of the ACLU of Southern California and the Public Law Center.

Susannah Nevison is the author of Teratology (Persea Books, 2015), winner of the Lexi Rudnitsky First Book Prize in Poetry New work can be found in, or is forthcoming from, *Crazyhorse*, *The National Poetry Review*, *Guernica*, and elsewhere. She is a 2016 Clarence Snow Fellow at the University of Utah, where she is a doctoral candidate.

Anne Richardson is the Director of the Consumer Law Project at Public Counsel, a non profit legal services organization in Los Angeles. Beginning in 2008, she represented a detainee in Guantanamo Bay, who was cleared and released in 2016.

Stephen Rohde is a constitutional lawyer, lecturer, writer and political activist. He is immediate past Chair of the ACLU Foundation of Southern California, Chair of Death Penalty Focus, a founder and Chair of Interfaith Communities United for Justice and Peace, and Chair Emeritus of Bend the Arc: a Jewish Partnership for Justice. Mr. Rohde is the author of the books American Words of Freedom and Freedom of Assembly and co-author of Foundations of Freedom published by the Constitutional Rights Foundation. He has written for the *Los Angeles Times*, the *Los Angeles Daily Journal* and the *Los Angeles Review of Books*. For over 45 years, he practiced law first in New York and then in Los Angeles, specializing in communications and intellectual property law, civil and appellate litigation and constitutional and civil rights law.

Natalie Shapero is the Professor of the Practice of Poetry at Tufts University and an editor at large of the *Kenyon Review*. Her poetry collections are *Hard Child* and *No Object*. In addition to her work in poetry, Natalie holds a law degree and was previously a litigation fellow with Americans United for Separation of Church and State.

Jonathan Shapiro is a former federal prosecutor. His first novel, *Deadly Force*, was released in April 2016. He is the co-creator and executive producer of the Amazon Prime series *Goliath*, and the author of *Lawyers, Liars and the Art of Storytelling*.

Mai Der Vang is the author of *Afterland* which received the Walt Whitman Award of the Academy of American Poets. Her writing has appeared or is forthcoming in *Poetry*, *Virginia Quarterly Review*, *New Republic*, *New York Times*, *Washington Post*, and elsewhere. She is co-editor of *How Do I Begin: A Hmong American Literary Anthology*. Mai Der has received residencies from Hedgebrook and she is also a Kundiman fellow.

FEATURED ARTISTS

Seth Alverson is a painter based in Los Angeles. His work has been exhibited at the Art Palace, the White Box Gallery in New York, Fort Worth Contemporary Art Center, the Austin Museum of Art as well as many other galleries and museums throughout the country. In 2015, he received a Joan Mitchell Award for painters and sculptors.

Miriam Cahn (b. 1949, Switzerland) lives and works in Basel and Bergell (GR), Switzerland. Her works are included in the collections of museums all over the world, significant solo exhibitions have been held at the Kunsthalle of Basel, Musée la Chaux-de-Fonds, Kunstmuseum Bonn, Haus am Waldsee in Berlin, Kunsthaus of Zurich, Kunstverein of Hanover, Musée Rath of Geneva, Museum für Moderne Kunst Frankfurt, Tate Gallery in London, Museum of Modern Art of New York, Cornerhouse in Manchester. She was included in Documenta 7 in 1982 and represented Switzerland at the 41st Venice Biennial, in 1984.

Karl Haendel is an American artist who lives and works in Los Angeles, California. He has exhibited at institutions including the Wexner Center in Columbus, Los Angeles's Museum of Contemporary Art, the Aspen Art Museum, New York's Drawing Center, the Solomon R. Guggenheim Museum, the Art Institute of Chicago, among many others.

Jibade-Khalil Huffman is the author of three books of poems, *19 Names For Our Band* (Fence, 2008) and *James Brown is Dead* (Future Plan and Program, 2011) and *Sleeper Hold* (Fence, 2015). His art and writing projects have been exhibited and performed at many museums including MoMA/PS1 and the Hammer Museum.

Sanaz Khosravi was born in Tehran, Iran, in 1990. In 2007, at the age of 17, she moved to the United States. She is currently studying Practice of Art (BA) at the University of California, Berkeley. Sanaz's work aims to create imageries of femininity in the contemporary world. Her works confront the social issues while focusing on hope in everyday life. She uses the power of art to touch the hearts and minds of people in order to inspire social changes in her home country and around the world.

Becky Kolsrud lives and works in Los Angeles. She received her MFA from UCLA in 2012. She recently had a solo show of her work at TIF SIGFRIDS in Los Angeles. Her work has recently been included in group exhibitions at Foxy Production and Maccarone gallery, both in New York. Her upcoming solo exhibition at JTT Gallery (New York) will mark her third solo exhibition by the gallery, which also represents her work. Her work is in the collection of the Hammer Museum (Los Angeles) and was recently acquired by the Hall Foundation.

Anne Libby lives and works in New York. She received her BFA Rhode Island School of Design in 2009 and received her MFA from Bard College in 2016. Her recent solo shows include *Marrow into Moxie* at Night Gallery in Los Angeles, *Lilies Lamellae* at Metropolitan Structures in Baltimore and *Les Annelés* at Violet's Café, Brooklyn. Selected group exhibitions are: *A Dumb Sound, A Sweet Bell* at 315 Gallery, Brooklyn; *There is no fact as to whether or not P* at 247365, New York; *Tears On My Spiderroll* at Violet's Café, Brooklyn; *The Fishbone Diagram* at U.S. Blues, Brooklyn; *Make it Work* at Sam's Place, Brooklyn, NY, 2014.

Ragen Moss's work has been shown in solo exhibitions most recently at Ramiken Crucible, NY, Redling in Los Angeles, and LA><ART in Los Angeles. She holds an MFA from UCLA, a JD from UCLA and a BA from Columbia University, and is a practicing attorney.